ARCHITECTURE OF THE WESTERN RESERVE  1800–1900

ARCHITECTURE OF

THE WESTERN RESERVE
1800–1900

RICHARD N. CAMPEN
Illustrated with photographs by the author

THE PRESS OF CASE WESTERN RESERVE UNIVERSITY / CLEVELAND AND LONDON / 1971

This book was set in ten-point
Melior. It was composed by
Dayton Typographic Service,
Dayton, Ohio, printed by Great
Lakes Lithograph Company,
Cleveland, Ohio and bound by
American Publishers Press, Chicago, Illinois.
The paper is Mohawk
Superfine, manufactured by Mohawk
Paper Mills, Inc., Cohoes, New York.
The design is by Nan C. Jones.

 To Helen
without whose patient understanding this
work would not have been possible

FOREWORD

Like all other Americans, we in Ohio have been so occupied with the constructions of our times and the rearranging of our physical environment that we have all but forgotten about the labors of the architects and master builders who came before us. In recent years, however, whether it be the result of conscience or the vague feeling of rootlessness, we have begun to look about the world of Ohio and evaluate what, in terms of buildings and landscapes, we have inherited. There is much to be found in spite of our extraordinary ability to disrupt and destroy the work of our predecessors. Richard Campen's fresh look at the Western Reserve is testimony to this fact, even though intensive urbanization has erased so much of what was built before us.

It seems nothing less than astounding that so few published works on the architecture of Ohio have appeared in the past. A state well fitted with colleges and with schools of architecture could have documented its buildings and noteworthy civic designs. Yet aside from the works of I. T. Frary, limited in time and scope as they are, we have been virtually undiscovered. But now, if current events across the state are indicative, this drought of information and review is about to be concluded. *Architecture of the Western Reserve, 1800–1900* will be one of the major evidences of a renewed concern about the buildings around us and the conservation of architectural values.

A reappraisal of our early architecture and city planning carries with it no assumption that this was work of such consequence as to serve as a model for the growth we have ahead of us; technological advances emphatically forbid this. We search out the best in our past, rather, for a number of reasons: to know how we came to be; how we mastered materials and employed constructional tools; how we felt about the values of life at various moments in history. We are constantly reminded that a building, be it humble or grand, is a perfect and often lasting manifestation of the salient facts about a certain time in our past: a sculptured statement, expressing with relative permanency the ideals, the attitudes, the vitality and technological advancement of a period.

As we search through these pages, which show what we have built and demonstrate that admirable talent and dedicated concern for detail and architectural content were evident throughout our past, we are reminded of the transitory nature of all the works of man in the fluid circumstances of the 1970's. If we are to preserve a significant sampling of our past and the infinitely hard work which built it, piece by piece, we are going to need resources which will guide us and develop standards of judgment which can be applied to preservation, whether through public concern and persuasion or through legal instruments. Documentary evidence of our architecture that is worth saving is a part of this process. This book will serve this important need as well as delighting and rewarding the reader who shares a concern for this region and its history.

Robert C. Gaede, A.I.A.

CONTENTS

Acknowledgment

The author wishes to thank those persons, too numerous to mention, who have talked with him, written to him, or in other ways helped him obtain information on the buildings shown in this volume.

PREFACE

Not since the appearance of *Early Homes of Ohio,* by I. T. Frary, in 1936 has any work dealt with the distinguished and historic architecture of any major portion of this state. Professor Edmund Chapman's *Cleveland: From Village to Metropolis* is a fine and detailed work that gives some idea of the architectural history of Cleveland, but its concern is primarily urbanistic. Frary's book, after thirty-five years, has remained the best on historic Ohio architecture, the best source to which the student, the architectural historian, or the traveler can turn for descriptions and photographs. The present work is in one way more limited in scope than Frary's and in another way less so. Whereas Frary, though perhaps favoring the northeastern part of the state, covered the whole of Ohio, the present work confines itself to the delightful region usually known as the Western Reserve or, simply, as "the Reserve." On the other hand, while Frary's survey stopped at the end of the Greek Revival (that is, around 1850), the present work covers the entire Victorian period as well and even ventures into the post-Victorian period to show some of the later work of Charles Schweinfurth.

This, then, is an in-depth look at the architecture of the Western Reserve from the earliest pioneer days to the beginning of the present century— insofar as it remains to be seen. The author has intended neither a textbook nor a comprehensive catalogue, but rather a selective photographic survey, supported with general and specific information, of nineteenth-century architecture remaining in the Reserve. It is hoped that this volume will stimulate interest in and concern for what remains of the fine architectural heritage of this area and thus work, in one way, for its preservation and restoration. Since Frary's time many fine buildings have been lost through outright demolition or simple neglect, and many have been thoughtlessly remodeled. Had there been a more general appreciation of their beauty and uniqueness, less of this destruction would have happened. A particularly poignant example of the losses of recent years has been the demolition of many buildings by Jonathan Goldsmith, the architect-builder of Painesville in Lake County.

The best remaining work is to be found in the smaller communities, such as Kinsman and North Bloomfield in Trumbull County, or Norwalk and Milan in the "Firelands," where expansion and "progress" have been less ruthlessly destructive. In the countryside too, as one drives along, fine houses sometimes appear unexpectedly, such as "Ionia," built in 1828, north of East Claridon in Geauga County, or the Judge Taylor house nearby. It is a thrill to come upon houses such as these, stately relics of a former era of taste and quality, both in the architecture of the Reserve and in that of the nation as a whole. How great our decline has been since, the real-estate sections of our newspapers testify.

Cleveland, the largest city of the region, is another matter. As the chief commercial center of the Western Reserve, it was by 1850 a prosperous city; little, however, survives of its good early and mid nineteenth-century architecture. Its rapid growth, which made possible such streets of mansions as Euclid Avenue on the East Side and Franklin Street on the West Side, was also the eventual cause of their decay and obliteration. Cleveland has not had a great avenue since.

A comparison with Connecticut, the parent state of our region, is interesting. In the course of working on this book, the author made an all-too-short trip through Connecticut to compare the early homes there with those of the Western Reserve. A whole summer would be needed to do justice to everything, and the author could observe carefully only Stonington, Canterbury, Pomfret, Suffield, Farmington, Litchfield, and adjacent areas. Contrary to what one might suppose, distinguished early homes are no commoner in Connecticut than they are in the Western Reserve. At the same time, however, the architectural heritage there seems to be more secure; expansion, even in the smaller communities, seems to threaten them less, and people are more inclined to understand and preserve their architectural heritage. Another impression was that the Victorian period had more of an effect on the appearance of the Reserve, a rapidly developing region at the time, than it did in the Nutmeg State.

Not infrequently one hears references to a "Western Reserve" style of architecture. In truth, there is no such style. The houses that seem to be examples of such are two-storied, often with the gable end of the roof facing the road, and with a one-storied wing that includes a recessed porch. This type of house, however, is not peculiar to the Reserve, and may in fact be found in many parts of the Midwest. It is, however, important in the local vernacular, and occurs with great frequency along the roads and in the smaller towns.

Finally, a word about this book and its organization. Often as the story has been told, even natives are in many cases uncertain as to what counties are included in the Western Reserve and how it came into being. We begin, therefore, with a brief historical sketch intended to summarize the essential facts.

The major part of the book follows. This is a section of nearly 400 photographs of existing Western Reserve buildings with descriptive captions, some short, some lengthy. The buildings are grouped by county, and each county division has its own brief historical introduction. Architectural interest, rather than mere venerability, was the principal criterion of choice, and many good but in one way or another typical buildings have had to be eliminated as well. Some "heritage" and "century" buildings have thus been left out as lacking in sufficient architectural interest. On the other hand, certain buildings with historic associations, such as "Lawnfield" (Mentor, Lake County), the last home of President and Mrs. James A. Garfield, have been selected over other buildings of the same type.

Realizing that many of his readers will not have had Art History 101, the author has added a short account of Western Reserve architecture in the context of the architectural history of the nation as a whole. This is followed by an illustrated glossary of architectural terms and by a bibliography for the reader who wishes to study further.

ARCHITECTURE OF THE WESTERN RESERVE ❀ 1800–1900

HISTORICAL
INTRODUCTION

Those of us who are native to the region of northeastern Ohio known as the Western Reserve tend to take the existence of this as a distinct geographical entity for granted. In the expectation that this volume may have interest for persons beyond the borders of the Reserve, it seems best, however, to begin with some explanation of its origin and a definition of the area which it includes.

At the end of the Revolutionary War, seven of the original thirteen states claimed lands extending westward to the Mississippi River or beyond, chiefly because of charters granted them by various sovereigns of England. Georgia, North Carolina, South Carolina, Virginia, New York, Connecticut, and Massachusetts were among these. Connecticut's claim stemmed from the charter granted by King Charles the Second on the twenty-third day of April, 1662, which defined its borders as follows:

Bounded on the East by the Narragansett River, commonly called Narragansett Bay, where the said River flows into the sea; on the North by the line of the Massachusetts plantation, on the South by the sea; and in longitude as the line of the Massachusetts Colony, running East and West, that is to say, from the said Narragansett Bay in the East to the South sea on the West [i.e., the Pacific Ocean], with the islands thereto adjoining.

The abandonment of these claims by the several states was the accomplishment of a Congress straining to obtain ratification of the Articles of Confederation. Maryland, which had stubbornly refused to sign until this matter was settled, accepted the Articles in 1781; North and South Carolina did not effect their transfers until 1790 and 1787 respectively. In making her cession in 1786, Connecticut reserved an extensive tract extending 120 miles west from the Pennsylvania border between 41 degrees and 42 degrees, 2 minutes, north latitude, and thus was allowed to retain a small portion of her western claims. This tract was then called, and has been known ever since, as the Western Reserve of Connecticut, or simply as the Western Reserve.* Connecticut, however, gave up political control of this area.

As early as 1786 plans were made by Connecticut authorities to survey

---

* Virginia also reserved land in Ohio; the Virginia Military Tract, between the Little Miami and Scioto rivers, was a reservation for war veterans.

this land and sell it to its citizens for the bargain price of six shillings per acre. However, the Northwest Territory, of which the Western Reserve was a part, was still a vast wilderness inhabited by Indians who were hostile because of the persistent incursions of the white man into their hunting lands. The Indians had not yet relinquished all claims to this territory, and had not even been a party to the peace treaty at the end of the War for Independence in which the British ceded it to the American colonies. The risks of widespread migration to, and settlement in, the region were deemed so great that by 1795—nine years later—only one sale had been made, a huge section in the vicinity of Youngstown comprising 24,000 acres and known as the Salt Spring Tract, to General Samuel H. Parsons.

Only after numerous inconclusive skirmishes and a disastrous defeat suffered by territorial governor Arthur St. Clair did General Anthony Wayne succeed in breaking the Indian power and bringing the red men to terms at the Treaty of Greenville (1795). The conditions of this treaty pushed the boundary of the Indian territory westward to the Cuyahoga and Tuscarawas rivers down to a point near Fort Laurens and west from there. Furthermore, General Moses Cleaveland, representing the Connecticut Land Company, which had purchased three million of the easternmost acres of the Western Reserve from the state of Connecticut for $1,200,000, met with chiefs of the Six Nations of the Iroquois at Buffalo Creek, near Lake Erie, before entering it early in the summer of 1796. He may have felt that he needed their compliance if he was to traverse the land safely and survey it.

The Land Company purchase included all territory east of the Cuyahoga River and Portage Path, a trail used by the Indians in crossing the height of land between the headwaters of the Cuyahoga (which flows into Lake Erie) and the Muskingum (which flows into the Ohio). General Cleaveland and his party were most careful to limit their activities in the summer of 1796 to lands east of the Cuyahoga and to respect the Indians' claim to the land beyond, which included a sizeable additional portion of the Western Reserve. Not until 1806, when most of the Indians were prevailed upon to relinquish their claim to all lands in Ohio, was the way opened for the settlement of the "Firelands," 500,000 acres at the western extremity of the Reserve that had been set aside by Connecticut to compensate the citizens of its towns who had been victims of wanton burning and destruction by British forces stationed in the New York area during the Revolutionary War. While the actual settlement of the Firelands commenced in 1809, it slackened greatly during the War of 1812 and did not really get under way until around 1815. The Firelands towns of Norwalk, North Fairfield, Greenwich, and New Haven take their names from counterparts in the mother state.

The Land Ordinance of 1785 established the "rectilinear system" for surveying the western lands. According to this system, a base line is established running east and west. Meridians are then marked off at six-mile intervals perpendicular to the base line. Finally, lines parallel to the base line are marked off at six-mile intervals, thereby establishing blocks or townships of thirty-six square miles. A tier of townships between meridians is referred to as a range. The subdivisions of the townships into areas one mile square are known as sections. This system was followed by Cleaveland and his party when they commenced the not inconsiderable task of surveying the Connecticut Land Company's holdings in the summer of 1796. However, for some unexplained reason, they laid out the meridians and the east-west lines only five miles apart to form townships having areas of only twenty-five square miles. The base line, running east and west just a few miles south of Youngstown, runs along the present-day Western Reserve Road. It generally follows the interconnected southern boundaries of the counties of Portage, Medina, and Huron. The Firelands embraced the present counties of Huron and Erie.

Although from the very beginning the city of Cleveland was intended as the commercial and political center of the Western Reserve—a vision which has certainly been realized—in the earliest years Warren, in Trumbull County adjacent to the Pennsylvania state line, was its capital. In a most readable and informative book, *The Western Reserve: The Story of New Connecticut in Ohio*,* Harlan Hatcher gives us this insight into the pioneer character of the two settlements:

Captain Ephraim Quimby, proprietor of Warren, built his cabin there in 1799. By the end of the next year there were sixteen white settlers in Warren. Moses Cleaveland's city at the mouth of the Cuyahoga was faring poorly in those first years—Turhand Kirtland, as field agent for the Company, wrote to General Moses Cleaveland from Cleveland on July 17, 1800 to report that Major Spafford, Lorenzo Carter and David Clark were the only inhabitants of the City.

Hatcher tells us that the itinerant Rev. Joseph Badger noted in his diary in 1800 that:

he found in Vienna only one family; in Hartford, three; Vernon, five; Warren and Canfield, eleven each; one at the "salt works"; five each at Deerfield, Boardman and Poland; seven at Mesopotamia; three at Windsor; one at Nelson; and two or three at Mantua. He does not say how many there were at Hudson, but on the Fourth of July thirty people gathered to hear Benjamin Tappan of Ravenna give the oration—as he rode north, he found five families at Newburgh; two at Cleveland; one each at Euclid and Chagrin; four at Mentor; two at Painesville; an unspecified number at Burton and Aurora; and two each at Harpersfield and Austinburg.

The above-mentioned communities are still among the many attractive villages and towns waiting to be explored by the architectural enthusiast who ventures over the less travelled roads of this delightful section, which has not received the attention it deserves.

* Passages from this book are reproduced by permission of the Bobbs-Merrill Co.

THE BUILDINGS
OF THE WESTERN
RESERVE

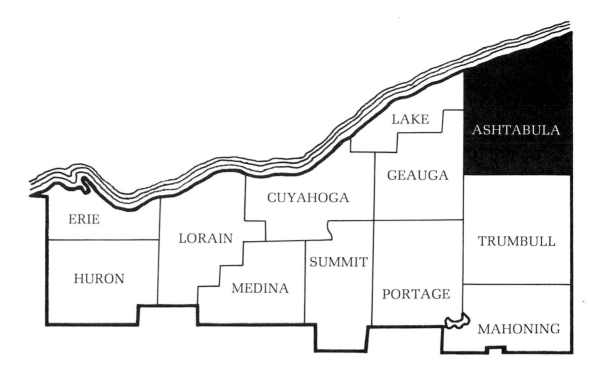

ASHTABULA COUNTY

Ashtabula County was erected in 1808 and organized in 1811 from Trumbull and Geauga counties. The name stems from the Indian word meaning "fish river." Moses Cleaveland's surveying party first touched the Western Reserve at the mouth of Conneaut Creek on July 4, 1796. The first white settler in the Western Reserve was Judge James Kingsbury, who arrived with his family shortly thereafter and built a cabin at Conneaut. The hardships endured by this family during the first winter, which included the death by starvation of the first white child born in the Reserve, are legendary. The first regular settlement in the county was at Harpersfield, March 7, 1798, by Alexander Harper and several associates from Harpersfield, New York. The county may boast today of having one of the best examples of an early Western Reserve home remaining to us intact, "Shandy Hall," the residence of Colonel Robert Harper, now maintained by the Western Reserve Historical Society.

Except for the lakeshore corridor, Ashtabula County remains rather sparsely populated and relatively unspoiled. The two most rewarding towns for architectural study are Jefferson, the county seat, and nearby Austinburg. Jefferson, always a small community, is remarkable for having produced two outstanding statesmen, Congressman Joshua R. Giddings and Senator Benjamin F. Wade, and for being the home town of the important jurist Rufus P. Ranney and the well-known author William Dean Howells. Unfortunately the Wade home, which stood near the center of town, was demolished in 1968 to make way for commercial expansion. Wade's law office, while lost to Jefferson, has been incorporated into the Pioneer Village complex being developed by the Western Reserve Historical Society at the Hale Homestead in Summit County. The substantial Giddings home is sadly neglected, but his separate law office remains to be seen in Jefferson. The principal charm and interest of Jefferson is in the public buildings and the fine old homes lining West Jefferson Street.

Austinburg, through the generosity of Joab Austin, became in 1835 the site of the Ashtabula County School of Science and Industry (now

Covered Bridge,
Doyle Road, Mill Creek
Of eighteen covered bridges in the entire Western Reserve, fifteen are in Ashtabula County.

the Grand River Institute). Its most famous landmark is "Sycamore Hall," the home of Eliphalet Austin, a founder. Another of Austinburg's claims to fame is that its Congregational church, the first in the Western Reserve, was organized in 1801 by the Rev. Joseph Badger, the first itinerant preacher in the Reserve.

A rewarding motor route in Ashtabula County is the Kelloggsville-Stanhope Road from its northern end, south and slightly west of Conneaut, southward to Kinsman, a couple of miles below the county line. A "find,"

a delight to come upon, is the old Stagecoach Inn at Kelloggsville.

Of eighteen covered bridges in the Western Reserve, fifteen are in Ashtabula County. The circuit of these, which can be accomplished in a leisurely day, is a rewarding experience. For this purpose it is recommended that the reader obtain a copy of a map, *Covered Bridges of Ohio,* published by the Ohio Historical Society, Columbus. Many of the other structures included in the photographic section of this volume will be encountered in the course of such a tour.

1. Covered Bridge, Route 21
Grand River at Eaglesmere
Fifteen of the eighteen covered bridges remaining in the Western Reserve are in Ashtabula County. There is more than meets the eye in the construction of these bridges, which attest to the skill and knowledge of these early "engineers."

2. Tyler House (c. 1835)
Federal
North State Street, Ashtabula
This lovely portico of a once-lovely residence is on Ashtabula's main street. The highly developed doorway, Federal in design, is like many that line Benefit Street in Providence, Rhode Island.

3

3. Law Row (after 1850)
Jefferson
Law Row, close to the Ashtabula
County courthouse, looks more like a
railroad station than attorneys' offices.

4. Joshua Giddings Law Office (1823)
Federal
Jefferson
At one time a lawyer or a doctor might
have his office in a small building
like this one, close to but separate
from his home.

5. Joshua Giddings Law Office.
Detail of doorway.

6. Ashtabula County Courthouse
(1850, 1891)
Jefferson
John Woolly, architect (1891 alteration)
The incised stone block above the
porch provides the dates of several
courthouses that have previously
occupied this site. The present building
is a remodeling of a handsome 1850
Greek Revival structure that was
surmounted by a square cupola with
paired corner pilasters. In the
foreground is a Civil War memorial,
executed by F. E. Smith.

7. Ashtabula County Courthouse.
Porch.

4

5

6

7

8. Probate Court Building (1870)
Bracketed
Jefferson, near courthouse
Levi T. Scofield, architect
Plans for this Victorian building were submitted in March 1870 by the Cleveland architect, best known for Cleveland's Soldiers' and Sailors' Monument. The date stone bears the inscription "1870 / J. M. Waters." Since there is no record of payment, it is assumed that Waters, a prominent builder, may have donated the building to the county. The metal awning does not enhance its appearance.

9

10

9. Obel-McCall House (1857)
Greek Revival
West Jefferson Street, Jefferson
An impressive late Greek Revival
house with symmetrical wings.
The two-bay portico is unusual, and
the pediment exceptionally bold.

10. 175 West Jefferson Street (c. 1855)
Tuscan
Jefferson
A stately interpretation of the
bracketed Italianate style.

11. 137 West Jefferson Street
Tuscan
Jefferson
Evidently by the same builder who did
number 175, shown in the previous
picture. The porch, however, is an
addition of the 1870's or '80's, and the
large window behind is obviously a
remodeling.

12. First Congregational Church (1877)
Gothic Revival
Austinburg
Rev. John Nutting, designer
This handsome Gothic Revival church
required two years to build. The
designer, a cousin of artist Wallace
Nutting, drew the plans, designed
all decorative detailing, and did much
of the construction work with his
own hands.

11

ASHTABULA COUNTY   15

13

14

15

16   ASHTABULA COUNTY

13. "Sycamore Hall" (1840–60)
Tuscan
Austinburg
For some reason the date 1815 is repeatedly given for this essentially Victorian residence but obviously such a refined house could not be an Ohio contemporary of "Shandy Hall" (p. 26). A mid-century date is much more plausible.

14. "Sycamore Hall." The ornate rear wing.

15. C. M. Pelton Store (c. 1826)
Greek Revival (except for wing)
Austinburg
The Pelton store is a fine example of an early general store in the Western Reserve. It is said to have been built in 1826 by Eliphalet Austin, founder of the town.

16. E. F. Brown House (1882)
Victorian
Kingsville
The nicest porch in Kingsville. The entrance lintel states that the house was built in 1882. Observe the delicate deck comb.

17. E. F. Brown House. Incised stone lintel.

18   ASHTABULA COUNTY

18. John Olmstead House (1878)
Tuscan/French
769 West Main Street, Conneaut
Built by John Olmstead after an oil
"strike" in Pennsylvania, this stately
Victorian residence now serves as
a museum of agricultural machinery.
Its most outstanding feature is the
mansard-roofed tower, from which
lake shipping could be seen. Drinking
water was collected in a basement
cistern.

19. Keith Stevens House (1896–97)
"Shingle Style" (in brick)
884 West Main Street, Conneaut
The rounded bay, with its modified
conical roof, suggests a pilothouse on a
lake ship. The composition and
detailing show the mingling of styles
often found in houses of the 1890's.
The interior joinery is of choice
woods, and the third floor has a huge
ballroom. In the basement is a 2,000-
gallon tank for rain water. John J.
Cummins, the original owner, was
president of the Pittsburgh and
Conneaut Dock Company.

20

20. Church of Christ (c. 1840)
Greek Revival
Hartsgrove
This church has lost the characteristic
ornamentation of its tower.

21

22

23

24

20   ASHTABULA COUNTY

21. Old Stagecoach Inn (1824)
Federal
Kelloggsville
Caleb Blogett, builder
This fine early Federal building has
been largely overlooked by
architectural enthusiasts. Records
indicate that the last coach stopped
here in 1852, just at the time when the
railroads began operation. The
"carport" is a late addition.

22. Old Stagecoach Inn.
The kitchen at the south end of the
inn still contains its old fireplace
and dutch oven.

23. Old Stagecoach Inn.
One of the two fine Federal
doorways.

24. Old Stagecoach Inn.
Bedroom fireplace.

25. 4743 Kelloggsville-Stanhope Road
Greek Revival (transitional)
Kelloggsville
This once-fine home, dating from the
1820's, suffered for many years
from an incongruous front porch which
hid its Greek entrance. A new
indignity, aluminum siding, is being
inflicted upon it.

26

27

26. Edmiston-Bishop House (c. 1845)
Greek Revival
West Andover
Leverett Osborn, builder

No one interested in the early architecture of the Western Reserve could pass this delightful little house without giving it more than a casual glance. The design is quite unusual.

27. Edmiston-Bishop House. Detail.

28. Osborn-Carpenter House (1843)
Greek Revival
4431 Kelloggsville-Stanhope Road,
Leon
Leverett Osborn, builder
This house, another Osborn design, is similar in plan to the Edmiston-Bishop house. Between the first-floor ceiling and the cupola room is a space three feet high, built for "underground railroad" fugitives and able to hold a dozen men. This house is in bad repair, and its future is doubtful.

29. Hegley-Pelen House (c. 1860)
Route 534 south of Windsor
The sides of this, the largest octagon house in Ashtabula County, are eighteen feet long. Each floor has four square and four triangular rooms. The large center hall is curved at the inner end, where a stair winds upward to the cupola.

30

31

30. House on Ohio Route 45, south of
U.S. Route 6
Victorian
Rome
Our disintegrating heritage. What
prosperous farmer took pride in this
now-crumbling residence?

31. Board-and-Batten House
Carpenter Gothic
Windsor Mills Road, West of
Route 534
At the middle of the nineteenth
century, Andrew Jackson Downing
advocated board-and-batten
construction. Here it is combined with
a riot of jigsaw work.

32

33

32. House on Phelps Road, south of
U.S. Route 322
Carpenter Gothic
Windsor Mills
This delightful bit of Victoriana comes
into view if one turns south onto
Phelps Road, as one does to visit the
covered bridge over the Grand
River, a short distance away.

33. Christ Episcopal Church (1832–34)
Greco-Gothic
Windsor Mills
Here, as at Claridon and elsewhere,
Greek and Gothic forms are combined.
This church, faithfully restored in
1964, is only one of the architectural
delights awaiting the traveler
through this sparsely populated region.

26   *ASHTABULA COUNTY*

34. "Shandy Hall" (1815)
Vernacular
Unionville
Col. Robert Harper, builder
Owned and administered by the
Western Reserve Historical Society,
this is one of the oldest homes of
the Reserve. The original house,
consisting of four rooms divided by a
central hall, was erected by Colonel
Robert Harper, whose father had come
to Harpersfield in 1798. The original
kitchen, with its brick fireplace and
oven, is in the basement.

35. "Shandy Hall."
Ten or eleven years after the
completion of the original portion of
the house, this banquet room was
added at the rear. Its dimensions are
32 by 16 feet, and it has a coved
ceiling. The hand-painted wallpaper
was bought from a bankrupt Buffalo
hotel.

36. Warner House (1835?)
Classic Revival
2052 County Line Road, Unionville
Jonathan Goldsmith, builder (?)
This doorway is so much like those by
Goldsmith in Painesville, Willoughby,
and elsewhere as to make it virtually
certain that this brick house too is by
him.

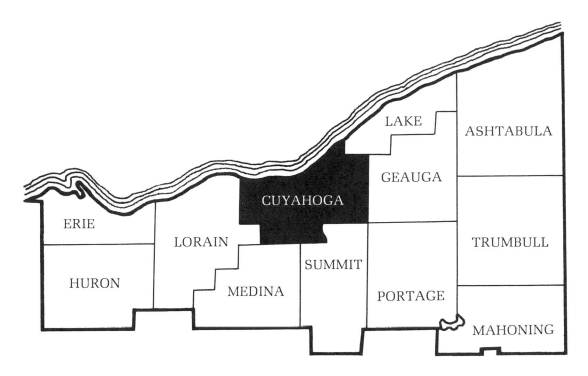

CUYAHOGA COUNTY

Cuyahoga County was erected in 1808 and organized in 1810 from Geauga County. The city of Cleveland thus antedates Cuyahoga County; it was founded on the 22nd of July, 1796, by Moses Cleaveland and a party of surveyors who moored their boat on the east shore of the Cuyahoga River not far from the site of St. Clair Avenue. Cleaveland conceived of the city as the commercial hub and capital of the Western Reserve. (The city, however, was slow to develop because of the marshy character of the land at the mouth of the river and its infestation with mosquitoes.) A principal feature of the plan of the town, drawn up by Amos Spofford and dated October 1, 1796, was Public Square, embracing ten acres of land, from which most streets were to radiate. Superior Avenue, which today bisects the Square, was planned to be the principal thoroughfare and indeed remained so until the present century, lined as it was by banking, commercial, and hotel facilities from the bluff by the river to the Square. As late as 1820 the population of Cleveland was estimated to be somewhat over 600 persons; by 1830, though, it was 1,075; by 1840 it stood at 6,071; and at mid-century it had soared to 17,034. The completion of the Ohio Canal in 1827 gave the first impetus for this rapid growth.

In these early days the social and political life of the city pulsated around Public Square. The finer homes of the more successful citizens were either built on the perimeter of the Square or close by. Harlan Hatcher, in *The Western Reserve: The Story of New Connecticut in Ohio*, graphically describes the scene which prevailed in 1840:

In the Public Square at Cleveland, cows leaned against the new, whitewashed fences which the City fathers had erected to keep them off the grass. The railings divided the Square into four sections. The little trees which had just been set out along the fences were protected by rails stood on end, wigwam style. The freshly whitewashed brick courthouse, two stories high, with a railing around its cornice and a big Ionic wood belfrey rising high above the roof, looked out over the trees towards the lake from the southwest quadrangle of the Square, where the statue of Moses Cleaveland now surveys his City.

Cleveland, the Metropolis of the Western Reserve
The Cuyahoga River and the High Level Bridge, seen from the Superior Viaduct

1

1. Old Stone Church (1853, 1857, 1884)
Romanesque
Public Square, Cleveland
Heard and Porter, architects

A church has occupied this corner since the earliest days of the city. The present church, replacing a stone structure of 1832, was first built in 1853 but was severely damaged by fire in 1857, at which time the interior was rebuilt. Heard and Porter were the architects in both instances. The interior was gutted once again in 1884, when Charles Schweinfurth was called upon to rebuild the church. Its side walls have thus withstood two devastating fires. "Old Stone" is the oldest structure in the city center. The roof is supported by hammer-beam trusses. Between 1868 and 1884 the right tower was capped with a spire which soared to a height of 238 feet, but this was later removed and never rebuilt. Many of the church's windows were designed and executed in the studios of Louis Comfort Tiffany.

The second courthouse, to which Mr. Hatcher makes reference, was from the standpoint of the architectural historian the most significant structure in the city at this period. Edmund Chapman, in his *Cleveland: Village to Metropolis* discusses the structure at some length and describes it as being in the Federal style. What a gem it would be if it remained for us today: but alas, it was torn down in 1858.

One of the earliest carpenter-builders of any significance of whom we have any knowledge was Hezekiah Eldredge, the builder of St. John's Historic Episcopal Church and a number of other structures in the then-separate community known as Ohio City, on the west bank of the Cuyahoga. The first architectural firm of any importance in Cleveland was the partnership of Simeon Porter, from Hudson, and Charles W. Heard, from Painesville, which existed from 1849 to 1859. However, few of the important buildings and homes attributable to this partnership remain in Cleveland.

Cleveland underwent a transformation from a purely mercantile town, as it was prior to the Civil War, into one of the most important centers of manufacturing in the nation during the final third of the nineteenth century. By the end of that century, Euclid Avenue was famous around the world for the quality of the homes which lined it almost to Doan's Corner

3

(East One Hundred Fifth Street), but particularly for those between Public Square and East Fortieth Street. Even so, as recently as 1906 the Cleveland Trust Company was considered by many to be misguided for establishing its main banking office as far east as East Ninth Street.

By any measure Charles Schweinfurth, who came to Cleveland in 1883, was the most significant architect to practice in Cleveland during this period. His homes and other structures, frequently executed in heavy rusticated ashlar, were inspired by the Richardsonian Romanesque style. Schweinfurth's career spilled over into the present century, and many of the important works for which he is noted and which remain to this day, such as Trinity Cathedral, at Twenty-second Street and Euclid Avenue, and the Samuel Mather residence, at 2605 Euclid Avenue, were executed after 1900; we have decided to show a few of these all the same. It is unfortunate that so much of his earlier work has been swept aside, but Euclid Avenue has changed from the fine residential street that it once was to the grim commercial thoroughfare that it is today.

If one wishes to seek out the earliest architecture of Cuyahoga County, one must look mostly to the smaller communities outside the great sprawling city which have as yet been more fortunate in evading the uncaring encroachment of the developers.

2. Soldiers' and Sailors' Monument (finished 1894)
Victorian
Public Square, Cleveland
Levi Scofield, architect and sculptor

The Monument was the labor of love of Levi T. Scofield, who was from one of Cleveland's pioneer families. A soldier and officer in the Union Army, he became an architect and sculptor. The central shaft of black Quincy granite and bronze, weighing 140 tons, attains a height of 125 feet and is surmounted by a bronze statue of Liberty, personified as a young woman. The Monument is most notable for the four, highly realistic, sculpture groups executed by Scofield, honoring the four branches of military service. At the north end of the Square one sees the Old Stone Church and the Society National Bank Building.

3. Soldiers' and Sailors' Monument. Sculpture group.

4. Society National Bank
Building (1890)
Gothic
Public Square, Cleveland
Burnham and Root, architects
Another of Cleveland's most venerable
landmarks is the Society National
Bank Building, originally the Society
for Savings Building, for which the
well-known Chicago firm of Burnham
and Root were architects. There is
some question as to whether this
massive stone "skyscraper" is the last
great structure in the city with
load-bearing walls, though it is known
that some iron was used in its
construction. Originally a great open
well, covered by a vast skylight,
provided daylight illumination
throughout the full height of the
building. The fenestration is varied
by two tiers of giant arches each three
floors high. The influence of
Richardson may be seen in certain
features: the rock-faced ashlar, the
squat, massive columns at the first
floor level, the turrets at the
upper corners, and the rounded arches.

5. Society National Bank Building.
The entranceway.

6. Society National Bank Building.
The corner lantern, fabricated by
Winslow Brothers of Chicago.

7. Society National Bank Building. The interior, with murals (1890) by the English illustrator and decorative artist Walter Crane.

8. The Perry-Payne Building (1888) Superior Avenue at West Ninth Street, Cleveland
Cudell and Richardson, architects
When completed in 1888, the Perry-Payne Building was the last word in commercial architecture—at least in Cleveland. Builders and architects from near and far came to inspect it and to marvel at the great inner court covered by a vast expanse of glass. Immediately the building became the headquarters for the lake shipping and iron companies forming the base of Cleveland's economy.

9. The Arcade (1890)
Romanesque Revival
412 Euclid Avenue, Cleveland
Smith and Eisenmann, designers and engineers
The Arcade is generally considered to be the most distinguished building of the city center. Extending 300 feet between Euclid and Superior Avenues, it was conceived as a great complex of shops and offices. The arcade proper is an interior passage 60 feet wide and 90 feet high, with a glass roof supported by iron trusses. Outside, the influence of Richardson is apparent, particularly in the great archway, once the main entrance, on the Superior Avenue front. The rock-faced arch, which springs from ground level, is an impressive feature. The Euclid Avenue entrance, once similar, was unfortunately remodeled in the 1940's. The interesting fenestration is also Richardsonian. George H. Smith and John Eisenmann, the latter a civil engineer at the Case School of Applied Science, were the engineers and designers for the structure, which cost $876,000.

10. The Arcade. Most of the original interior embellishments are still present: the ornate brass newel posts, the wrought-iron railings, and the lamp posts, along with harmonious ornamentation added at a later date. Unfortunately, the original bluish-gray mosaic floor has been replaced.

11. The Arcade. View of roof trusses.

CUYAHOGA COUNTY   35

12. Garfield Memorial (1890)
Romanesque Revival
Lakeview Cemetery, Cleveland
George Keller, architect
Also dedicated in 1890 was this
monument commemorating President
James A. Garfield, of Mentor, Ohio,
who had been assassinated in the
summer of 1881. The building is in the
form of a circular tower 50 feet in
diameter and 180 feet tall, preceded by
a rectangular entrance and vestibule.
The forms are again Romanesque. The
plan is that of George Keller of
Hartford, Connecticut, whose design
was selected from an international
competition in which 50 entrants,
including Charles Schweinfurth,
participated. The interior is splendidly
decorated with marble and mosaics.

13. Garfield Memorial. Realistic
bas-reliefs depicting episodes in the
life of the President. The sculptor was
Casper Buberl.

14. St. John's Historic Episcopal
Church (1836)
Gothic Revival
Church Avenue, Cleveland
Hezekiah Eldredge, builder
It is curious that this, the oldest
surviving church in Cleveland, built in
1837 at the very height of the nation's
enchantment with the Greek Revival,
should have been executed in the
Gothic Revival style. The profile of the
church suffers greatly by the loss of
the pinnacles at the four corners of the
central tower and upon the flanking
turrets. Designed and built by
Hezekiah Eldredge, who had migrated
to "Ohio City" only a year or two
previously from Rochester, New York,
St. John's has associations with many
early Clevelanders, including members
of the Rhodes, Castle, Norton, and
Hanna families, whose marriages are
commemorated in stained glass. With
the exception of minor alterations
and repairs, necessitated by a
damaging tornado in the early 1950's,
the church remains intact.

15. St John's Historic Episcopal
Church. Entrance.

14

15

CUYAHOGA COUNTY   37

16. Detroit-Superior Viaduct (1878)
Cleveland

When this bridge was completed, in 1878, Clevelanders thought that the problem of bridging the river and the adjacent Flats, which are well below the general downtown level, was solved for all time. How could they have realized that the growth of the city would, a mere three decades later, make a new and greater bridge —the once-famous High Level Bridge —imperative? Prior to the building of the great viaduct, it had been necessary for Clevelanders to descend Superior Avenue to the river, cross the small rotary Center Street Bridge, then ascend Detroit Street to Pearl. Only the portion of the viaduct shown in the photo exists; the part that bridged the river and joined lower Superior Avenue was dismantled following the completion of the High Level Bridge in 1912. The stone, it is believed, came from quarries in the vicinity of Peninsula in northern Summit County. This vestige stands, a monument to the past, like a long disused Roman aqueduct.

17. Cleveland Grays Armory (1893–94)
Romanesque Revival
1234 Bolivar Road, Cleveland

One of the most picturesque buildings in downtown Cleveland, but one to which little attention is paid, is the home of the Cleveland Grays, the first military organization in the city. The building suggests a medieval fort, with its massive round tower, machicolated at the top and fitted with slits behind which one might imagine defenders crouching with aimed crossbows. Also impressive is the Romanesque entranceway, with its massive arch of rock-faced voussoirs. Within the armory is a great drill hall and gymnasium which served for many years as a community assembly hall and sports arena. The armory was dedicated in May 1893 and completed in 1894.

18. Dunham Tavern (1832)
Vernacular
6709 Euclid Avenue, Cleveland
Built in 1832 as a home and shortly
thereafter becoming a stage stop,
Dunham Tavern is the oldest
structure in the central city. Forms of
the Greek Revival appear in the front
entrance and in the recessed porch in
the far wing; however, the house could
hardly be cited as a convincing
example of the style. Today, the
Tavern is operated as a museum
depicting the early life of the settlers
and is open to the public.

19

19. George Merwin House (Rowfant
Club) (c. 1850)
Tuscan Eclectic
3028 Prospect Avenue, Cleveland
George Merwin was an early resident
of Cleveland. Some of the materials in
this, his last residence, were said to
have been salvaged from his earlier
house on or near the Flats. The exact
construction date is not known, but it
seems quite reasonable to assume,
from its Victorian character, that it
was built after 1845. The Renaissance
window pediments, as well as the
pedimental treatment of the porch
roof, are highly unusual. Inside,
downstairs parlors flanking the center
hall each contain marble hearths and
mantels typical of the period. The
woodwork is heavy, with "rabbit ear"
offsets at the upper corners. A great
brick, floor-to-ceiling fireplace by
Charles Schweinfurth, a founding
member, dominates the tavern-like
dining hall, which extends the width
of the house behind the parlors. The
building has served the Rowfant Club
since 1895. Originally the house was
on a large plot fronting on Euclid
Avenue. Lying in the path of an
extension of Prospect Avenue, it was
moved southward earlier in this
century. The owners of the house after
Merwin were the Ackley and
Doubleday families: it was the latter
that sold it to the Rowfant Club.

20

20. Wade Memorial Chapel (1901)
Greek Revival
Lakeview Cemetery, Cleveland
Hubbell and Benes, architects

Although the Wade Memorial Chapel
was built in 1901, a year beyond the
time scope of this volume, it is such
a fine expression of the Greek
architecture with which we have been
so largely concerned that it is
impossible to pass it over. The
architects were Hubbell and Benes, the
same partnership which designed the
lovely Cleveland Museum of Art
(1916). The chapel stands as a
memorial to Jephtha H. Wade, early
Cleveland industrialist and founder of
the Western Union Telegraph
Company. It is open for the use of all
who wish to hold services and is
as beautiful within as it is from
without. This is not a slavish copy
of any known Greek temple, but a
modern adaptation of the Greek forms
to a present day use. The half columns
breaking the monotony of the
sidewalls are particularly successful.

21

But the outside is only half the story, for the interior walls of this temple are banded with colorful allegorical mosaics of great beauty, and the rear wall contains a Tiffany window of uncommon beauty. The "discovery" of this chapel by one who is prepared to understand it may evoke the same admiration one feels when standing before the Athenian Treasury at Delphi or the mosaics within St. Appolinare Nuovo at Ravenna. In short, it is a jewel!

21. Wade Memorial Chapel. Side view.

22. Calvary Presbyterian Church (1887–90)
Romanesque Revival
Euclid Avenue at East 79th Street, Cleveland
Charles F. Schweinfurth, architect
As in many of his nineteenth-century designs, Schweinfurth has used the Romanesque style. Note the narrow, round-headed openings, the great entrance archway, and the massive, crenelated twin towers.

23. Calvary Presbyterian Church. The recessed orders of the entrance arch and its stubby supporting columns are imitated from European prototypes.

24. Calvary Presbyterian Church. The 79th Street front of the church has a variety of arched windows of various sizes, gables, chimneys, and pinnacles. The Gothic fellowship hall, to the far left, was the first part of the complex to be built.

26

25. Charles Schweinfurth House (1894)
Romanesque Revival
1951 East 75th Street, Cleveland
Charles F. Schweinfurth, architect
One of the most interesting residences
still surviving by this architect is the
house that he built for himself.
Fortress-like, it is faced with
rock-faced masonry and capped with
crenelations.

26. Charles Schweinfurth House.
One's attention is immediately drawn
to the meticulously detailed arched
entrance. To the right is a
wrought-iron lantern, attached to a
shaft terminating in a corbel with the
motif of a lion and a shield—a
favorite motif of Schweinfurth's.

29

27. Charles Schweinfurth House. The interior as a whole is rather plain, but contains a number of details of the sort that one would expect of so cultured and imaginative a designer: stained-glass windows with architectural motifs, specially designed lighting fixtures, and stair balusters, rising nearly to the ceiling, that give the effect of a screen.

28. Charles Schweinfurth House. Parlor fireplace.

29. Charles Schweinfurth House. The great oak door with its strap-iron hinges, carved by the architect himself. The S-shaped door handle is noteworthy.

30. Franklin Backus Law School
Building (1896)
Renaissance Revival
Adelbert Road, Cleveland
Charles F. Schweinfurth, architect

This building, which houses the law
school at Case Western Reserve
University, is one of its architect's few
essays in classical design. It is built of
Ohio buff sandstone and has a hipped,
copper-covered roof. The ground floor
contains classrooms, and the upper
floor originally had a library to the
left of the central hall and a recitation
room to the right. Pinkish Ionic
columns support the entablature over
the entrance. The porch is lined with
golden-brown Roman brick.

31. Law School Building.
Entrance.

32. Mary Chisholm Painter Arch (1904)
Gothic
Flora Stone Mather College, Case
Western Reserve University, Cleveland
Charles F. Schweinfurth, architect

Few of those who pass daily through
this lovely arch are aware that it is by
Schweinfurth.

33

34

46   CUYAHOGA COUNTY

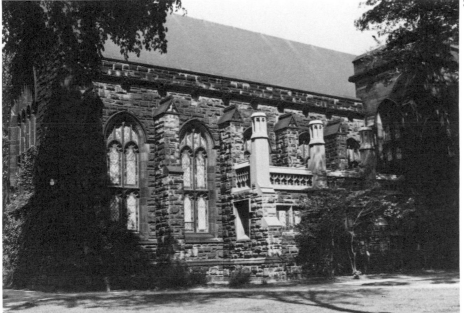

 36

33. Haydn Hall (1902)
Tudor
Flora Stone Mather College, Case
Western Reserve University, Cleveland
Charles F. Schweinfurth, architect
Yet another Schweinfurth design for
this campus.

34. Samuel Mather House (1907–10)
Tudor
2605 Euclid Avenue, Cleveland
Charles F. Schweinfurth, architect
By 1907, when Schweinfurth accepted
this commission from Samuel Mather,
he had abandoned Romanesque forms
in favor of Tudor. In so doing he
influenced the taste of wealthy
Clevelanders for the next few decades.
This former mansion is now a student
center for Cleveland State University.

35. Harkness Memorial Chapel (1902)
Gothic
Flora Stone Mather College, Case
Western Reserve University, Cleveland
Charles F. Schweinfurth, architect
Another essay in the Gothic style.

36. Harkness Chapel.
Interior.

37

37. Bridge (c. 1900)
Liberty Boulevard, Wade Park,
Cleveland
Charles F. Schweinfurth, architect
Much admired for the way in which it
fits its park setting and for the curving
stair.

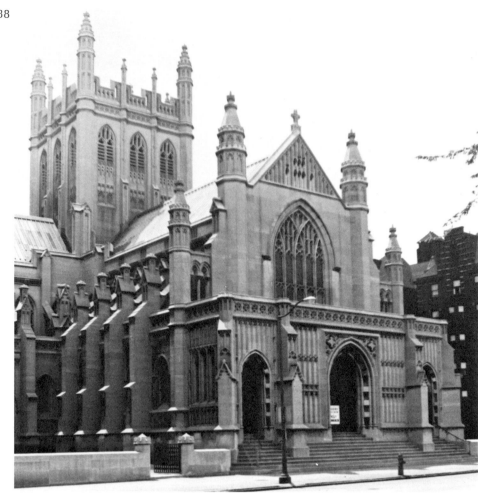

38. Trinity Cathedral (1901–07)
English Gothic
Euclid Avenue at East 22nd Street,
Cleveland
Charles F. Schweinfurth, architect
This, Schweinfurth's masterpiece, is
often considered the finest piece of
ecclesiastical architecture in
Cleveland. The original plans, made
shortly before the turn of the century,
were in the Romanesque Revival style.

39. Henry P. White House (1901)
Tudor
Euclid Avenue at East 90th Street,
Cleveland
Frank B. Meade, architect
This house, typical of those built by
prosperous Clevelanders at the turn of
the century, is one of the few
remaining on Euclid Avenue.
Fortunately, it is in good repair; it is
now used as a funeral home.

40. Henry P. White House. Porch.

41. Henry P. White House. Center hall.

42. Henry P. White House. Upstairs
study, with oriel seen in Figure 44.

43. Henry P. White House.
Parlor, first floor.

44. Henry P. White House. Oriel
overlooking stair landing.

39

40

41

42

43

44

45. John Honam House (1838)
Vernacular
14923 Edgewater Drive, Lakewood

It may very well be true, as claimed, that this is the oldest stone house in Cuyahoga County. When built it was located on Detroit Road, the main thoroughfare westward from Cleveland. In 1952, however, it was moved to Lakewood Park and converted into a museum of early pioneer living in the Western Reserve. The house is a very simple expression of the local vernacular.

46. Pomeroy House (1848)
Greek Revival
Village Square, Strongsville

Built in 1848 by Alanson Pomeroy, this house is a particularly fine example of the Greek Revival in brick. It takes the form of a central block with wings extending south and west. Its entrance has an overdoor light and side lights. This is the finest piece of early architecture in Strongsville, and it is to be hoped that local citizens will find the means to acquire it for public purposes. In 1964, however, only a concerted effort on the part of the "Friends of the Pomeroy House" prevented its replacement by a filling station. The builder, Alanson Pomeroy, came to the township in 1822 and, "beginning with nothing but his own skill, industry and integrity, . . . acquired considerable property through good management and perseverance."

47. Pomeroy House. The Doric doorway.

48. Town Hall, Brecksville (c. 1875)
Bracketed

Easily the most picturesque building of those encircling the village square at Brecksville is this town hall, now converted in part into a community playhouse. The paired eaves bracketing, the rounded stone window and door heads, the delightful octagonal rooftop cupola—all proclaim it to be a structure of the 1870's. A master plan calling for the expansion or possible replacement of this structure now threatens its existence. It is to be hoped that the citizens of Brecksville will have the good judgment to retain this landmark for the enjoyment of future generations.

49. George March House (c. 1845)
Greek Revival
126 East Washington Street,
Chagrin Falls

Chagrin Falls was founded in 1833, but this is believed to be the oldest extant building in the village. It is probably also the only Greek Revival building that has not been altered.

50. George March House.
East wing.

51. 178 High Street (c. 1875)
Carpenter Gothic
Chagrin Falls
Joe O'Malley, builder

52. Barn
Carpenter Gothic
48 Church Street, Chagrin Falls
Joe O'Malley, builder

For many years Joe O'Malley had a lumberyard and woodworking shop in Chagrin Falls. O'Malley was a master of the power-driven jigsaw, which came into use after the Civil War. Specimens of his imaginative and skillful workmanship are still to be found in the village, and the Western Reserve as a whole shows the work of such carpenters.

53. 177 South Main Street (c. 1875)
Carpenter Gothic
Chagrin Falls
Joe O'Malley, builder

54. O'Malley-Babinsky House (1872)
Carpenter Gothic
54 Church Street, Chagrin Falls
Joe O'Malley, builder

CUYAHOGA COUNTY   53

56

57

54   CUYAHOGA COUNTY

55. Stoneman-Nokes House (c. 1873)
Victorian
18 East Orange Street, Chagrin Falls
Chagrin Falls, a pleasant satellite of Cleveland located at the southeastern corner of the county, is essentially Victorian in its early architecture. One of the nicer Victorian homes in the village is the one pictured here, to which a date of circa 1873 has been assigned. The brick of which it is constructed—like all brick for homes of the period in the village—was made at the Boss Hutchings Brickyard, now gone, off Cleveland Street nearby. Note the cast grillwork decorating the door. There are many similar compositions in the village, but none of purer form.

56. Stoneman-Nokes House. Entrance.

57. Chagrin Valley Hunt Club
Gates Mills
Through this doorway many of Cleveland's wealthy have walked. The Federal-style house for which it was made was originally that of Holsey Gates, founder of Gates Mills. It is one of the few parts of the building to survive a fire in 1935.

58. St. Christopher's by the River (1853)
Greek Revival
Gates Mills
Holsey Gates, builder
Enhanced by a superb setting at the edge of the Chagrin River in the charming Western Reserve village of Gates Mills, St. Christopher's is easily one of the most attractive early churches in the region. Holsey Gates, who settled in this valley in 1826, originally leased the land on which the church stands to a Methodist congregation and put up $800 of the $1,300 required to build it in 1853. Episcopal services were first held in the church in 1906 and the Episcopal diocese finally acquired it in 1927. Although the octagonal cupola and spire are not in the Greek vocabulary, the building is essentially Greek Revival. The church was refurbished and modified under the supervision of the noted Cleveland architect Frank R. Walker in 1927–28. Each of the great windows flanking the entranceway contains thirty-six lights.

59. Holsey Gates House (1892)
Stick Style
762 Broadway, Bedford
Most travelers will pass the Gates house without a second glance. Its conically roofed corner towers, gables, front porch, and gingerbread work are outmoded. The perceptive traveler, however, finds this house an arresting vision. And the interior of this period piece is even more exciting. Oaken woodwork, beautifully preserved, and stained glass give it period charm and elegance. The builder was Holsey Gates, son of a gristmill owner in Chagrin Falls and grandson of the founder of Gates Mills.

60. Holsey Gates House. Main stair, showing hand-carved newelpost.

61. Holsey Gates House. Doorway between two parlors.

62. Holsey Gates House. Parlor mantelpiece.

63. Holsey Gates House. Dining room.

64. Holsey Gates House. Alcove in dining room.

60

65

65. Drake House (c. 1850)
Greek Revival
24262 Broadway, Oakland Village

This impressive late Greek Revival
house, located at a distance from the
road, was obviously the home of a
prosperous farmer. The Doric entrance
and pediment light, both framed in
native stone, are focal points of the
composition. An unusually fine
example of its period, it ought not to
be allowed to fall into disrepair.

66. Gilbert-Youmell House (c. 1855)
Greek Revival (transitional)
6344 SOM Center Road, Solon

The original builder of this
substantial late-Greek Revival house
could not have foreseen how it would
be shaken daily by the trains of the
Erie-Lackawanna Railroad, which pass
a few feet away. The house survives,
however, as an interesting example of
mixed Greek and carpenter Gothic
forms.

67. 33519 Solon Road (c. 1865)
Vernacular
Solon

The vergeboard and the Tudor
moldings over the windows impart
architectural character to a plain
house.

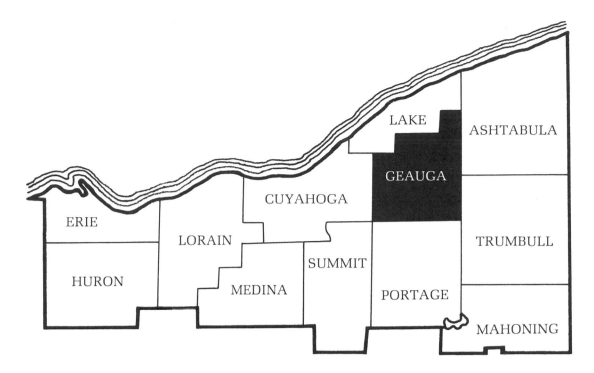

GEAUGA COUNTY

Geauga County, erected and organized in 1806 from Trumbull, was the second county to be established in the Western Reserve. The name stems from the Indian word for raccoon. Located for the most part on high ground and geographically situated so as to feel the maximum "lake effect," the county is noted for its deep winter snows; the settlers who came to Burton in 1798 hardly survived the first winter.

Geauga, despite the encroachments of suburbia, remains one of the most rural, and thus unspoiled, counties in the Western Reserve: Geauga County maple syrup is well known. Perhaps this is why the Amish have persisted in and about Middlefield and Parkman. Chardon and Burton, the two largest communities in the county, both reward persons in search of our architectural heritage. The town square at Chardon, with the Victorian courthouse at its northern end, is one of the most delightful in the Reserve. Of late there have been ominous signs of "progress" in the area of this common, and it is hoped that the community will have the good sense to direct any development so as to enhance the already pleasant scene.

Burton, site of the oldest county fair in the state and home of the Geauga County Historical Society, has for a decade been developing a Pioneer Village adjacent to its common with carefully selected architectural remnants salvaged from the countryside.

Architectural serendipity can be practiced along the byways of Geauga County with great profit. Awaiting the recognition of the tourist's admiring eyes are such fine specimens as the Charles B. Smith house, on State Road at East Claridon, the picturesque Greco-Gothic Church at Claridon, and the Judge Taylor House on Taylor-Wells Road. There are many, many others.

The Square, Chardon
The county courthouse, seen
through the trees

61

1. Geauga County Courthouse (1869)
Tuscan Bracketed
Chardon
Remove the cupola of this picturesque Victorian courthouse and a Tuscan villa remains.

2. Judge Taylor House (c. 1828)
Greek Revival
Taylor-Wells Road, north of Route 322
Charles B. Smith, builder (?)
A virtual duplicate of Smith's own house at East Claridon.

3. Charles B. Smith House (1828)
Greek Revival
State Road, East Claridon
Charles B. Smith, builder
Possibly this house was originally faced with flush siding as a foil to the pilasters. There was probably at one time an architrave over the capitals.

4. Elisha Parmlee House (1837)
Greek Revival
316 Water Street, Chardon
Charles B. Smith, builder (?)
The Ionic pilasters impart monumental quality to this otherwise simple front. The similarity of these capitals to work known to be by Smith suggests him as the builder of this house.

5

5. Congregational Church (1831)
Greek Revival
Route 322, Claridon

The twin entrances are a unique
feature among Greek Revival churches
in the Western Reserve. The Gothic
windows should be noted.

6. Congregational Church, Claridon.
Cornices and tower.

7. Congregational Church, Claridon.
Interior.

8. Thomas Levin House (1847)
Vernacular
Old State Road, near Lake County line
Thomas Levin, builder

One of the rare early stone houses
east of the Cuyahoga River.

9. Thomas Levin House.
Detail, showing tooling.

10. Williams-Bundy House (c. 1860)
Greek Revival
Parkman

Originally the home of a Dr. Williams,
who was killed in the Civil War, the
house was sold in 1875 to a Dr. Edwin
Bundy and is best known as the
"Bundy place." The pyramidal hip
roof is unusual. Construction is
unique. The walls are three bricks
thick and plastered inside without
furring. Foundation stones are three
feet long. And the roof is supported
by heavy trusswork.

CENTURY
HOME
BUILT
1847
BY
Thomas Levin

GEAUGA COUNTY 65

11. Doctor Goodwin House (c. 1825)
Federal
Burton
A date of 1814 has been given for this handsome house north of the town square. The author, however, believes this to be a decade too early. The parlor has noteworthy woodwork.

12. Methodist Church
Gothic Revival
Thompson
This small community at the northeast corner of Geauga County is the birthplace of Charles Martin Hall, inventor of the electrolytic process for refining aluminum.

13. George Boughton House (1834)
Federal
Pioneer Village, Burton
This entrance is a late survival of the Federal style into the Greek Revival period.

14. Church (1868)
Vernacular
Route 306 at Chagrin-Bainbridge Road, Bainbridge
C. O. Dutton, builder
The simple tower of this equally simple church is an addition.

GEAUGA COUNTY   67

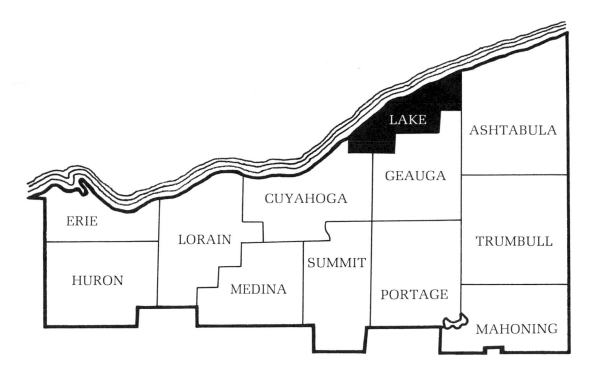

LAKE COUNTY

Lake County was erected and organized in 1840. It is one of the more rewarding counties of the Western Reserve for the architectural historian. This is so largely because of the legacy of fine early homes by the master builder Jonathan Goldsmith in Willoughby, Mentor, and Painesville. Important also are two works with which his son-in-law, Charles Wallace Heard, was associated, "Jennings Place" and "College Hall" at Lake Erie College, both in Painesville. The most important single building in the county is the Mormon Temple at Kirtland, from both a strictly historical and an architectural viewpoint. This was built by the dedicated members of the sect with the same fervor that motivated the builders of France's great Gothic cathedrals in the thirteenth century.

A structure of mainly historic value is "Lawnfield," at Mentor, the home of our nation's twentieth President, James A. Garfield. There are also two early stage stops, Lutz's Tavern at Painesville and the Unionville Tavern, the remains of one of the better octagon houses in the Reserve at Painesville, and several fine specimens of our earlier stone homes.

The Mormon Temple, Kirtland
A mixture of styles sometimes found
in Western Reserve churches

1

2

1. "Lawnfield" (1831, 1876)
Vernacular
Mentor Avenue, Mentor
James A. Garfield bought "Lawnfield" in 1876 and conducted his successful presidential campaign from its front porch. Of interest is a library with fine woodwork, begun in 1885 to designs by a Cleveland architect named Coburn.

2. Garfield Log Cabin (reconstruction)
"Lawnfield," Mentor
This reconstruction of the cabin in which Garfield was born is an example of the pioneer building in the Western Reserve.

3. Corning-White House (c. 1830)
Classic Revival
8353 Mentor Avenue, Mentor
Jonathan Goldsmith, builder
This house was built on a T-plan, greatly favored by Goldsmith. The symmetrical wings have had half-stories added to them.

4. Corning-White House. Doorway.

5

6

72   LAKE COUNTY

7

5. Sawyer-Wayside House (1843)
Vernacular
9470 Mentor Avenue, Mentor
Daniel Sawyer, builder
The neo-Georgian doorway is an incongruous addition to a plain but unusual stone house.

6. Heard-Minch House (1830?; demolished 1970)
9647 Mentor Avenue, Mentor
Jonathan Goldsmith, builder (?)
This house was supposedly built by Goldsmith and presented to his daughter and her husband Charles W. Heard on the occasion of their wedding. The side wings are obviously additions.

7. Joseph Sawyer House (c. 1820)
Greek Revival
9364 Forsythe Road, Mentor
Jonathan Goldsmith, builder
This early home has been moved from its original location at Mentor Avenue and Chillicothe Road. The exterior has been preserved, but the interior has been partly altered.

8

9

8. Joseph Sawyer House. The molded window frame with corner blocks, here with an oak-leaf motif, is typical of Goldsmith.

9. Mantel from Colonel Lemuel Storrs House (c. 1825–30)
Classic Revival
Lake County Historical Society, Mentor
Jonathan Goldsmith, builder
The Storrs house was a brick town house similar to the Morley house in Painesville. It would be difficult to improve on the simple classic lines of this mantelpiece.

10

10. Joseph Sawyer House. Doorway.

74   LAKE COUNTY

11. Dr. John Mathews House (1829)
Classic Revival
309 West Washington Street,
Painesville
Jonathan Goldsmith, builder
This is the best preserved and finest remaining example of Goldsmith's work. Basically Greek Revival in design and plan, it retains some Federal detailing. Again, the T-plan with symmetrical wings is used.

12. Dr. John Mathews House. Doorway.

13. Dr. John Mathews House. View from east.

14. Dr. John Mathews House. The semi-elliptical window in the pediment is Federal in style.

15. Dr. John Mathews House. Doorway from inside.

16. Dr. John Mathews House. Staircase.

17. Dr. John Mathews House. Mantelpiece, with portrait of Dr. Mathews.

18

18. "College Hall," Lake Erie College
(1859)
Tuscan
Painesville
Heard and Porter, architects
This, the last and largest project of
the Cleveland office of Heard and
Porter, is now the college
administrative building. The main
floor is supported by cast-iron
columns.

19. Dr. Everett Denton House (1816)
Classic Revival
55 Mentor Avenue, Painesville
Jonathan Goldsmith, builder
The Denton house is believed to be the
first in the Western Reserve by
Goldsmith. The original entrance has
unfortunately been replaced. The
house follows the custom of the
period in using flush siding on
the front, as a background for the
pilasters, and clapboard elsewhere.

20. Lutz's Tavern (1810–1818, 1832)
Vernacular
792 Mentor Avenue, Painesville
*Jonathan Goldsmith, builder
of 1832 portion*

Originally known as the Rider Tavern,
this was an early stagecoach stop on
the Buffalo-Cleveland Road. Believed
by local historians to have been
finished in its original form in 1818, it
received a full second story and the
present imposing portico from
Goldsmith. The primitive stone
foundation is of interest, but the
interior is not.

21. Uri Seeley House (c. 1830)
Late Federal
969 Riverside Drive, Painesville
Jonathan Goldsmith, builder (?)
While not positively attributed to
Goldsmith, the "ship construction" in
the roof is similar to that used in the
Denton and the Robinson-Elwell
houses. The attenuated pilasters also
suggest Goldsmith's hand.

22. Uri Seeley House. The doorway is
the most interesting detail of the
house, even though the original door
is missing.

19

LAKE COUNTY   77

23

25

23. City Hall (1840)
Greek Revival
Painesville
George Mygatt, builder (?)
Presently a portion of the Painesville city hall, this building was originally the Lake County courthouse. Early photographs indicated that the porch columns were originally square. A bronze plaque erroneously attributes the building to Goldsmith.

24. Octagon (Hobday-Walzer) House (1850)
Mentor Avenue, Painesville
Hobday, builder
Long admired, this house, now in a used car lot, is almost beyond hope. The brickwork is in Flemish bond. A central stair winds around the chimney. The octagon plan was promoted by Orson Fowler, a phrenologist from New York state, who claimed multiple advantages for it: freedom from dark corners; better exposure to sunlight in winter and cooling breezes in summer than the rectangular plan permits; and a maximum enclosure of space for a given amount of exterior wall. There is also an octagon house at Monroeville.

25. Octagon (Hobday-Walzer) House. Doorway.

26. Lewis Morley House (1836)
North State and East Jackson Streets,
Painesville
Jonathan Goldsmith, builder

In the design of this town house, Goldsmith seems to have been influenced by the handbooks of Asher Benjamin and others. Built at the height of the Greek Revival, it is definitely not Greek. Of particular interest is the way in which the walls are set off in panels by strips of brick. It is said that the front porch originally extended all the way across, but there are no marks on the masonry to indicate this.

27. Lewis Morley House.
Entrance.

28. Lewis Morley House.
Window in the south gable.

29. "Jennings Place."
Cast-iron porch balustrade.

30. "Jennings Place" (1869–72)
Tuscan
Casement Avenue, Painesville
Heard and Blythe, architects

It required almost three years to build this, the most pretentious Tuscan villa in Lake County. It was built by Charles Jennings for his daughter Frances, who married General Jack Casement, contractor for a portion of the Union Pacific Railroad. The house has a view of the Grand River.

LAKE COUNTY   81

31

32

33

34

35

31. St. James' Church (1866)
Gothic Revival
Painesville
Heard and Blythe, architects
St. James' Church is still in excellent condition, with all its finials in place, after over a hundred years. The interior has a dark wooden ceiling with carved pendants. The apse is framed in a great wooden arch simulating stone.

32. St. James' Church. Entrance.

33. Doorway (1870's?)
Carpenter Gothic
U.S. Route 20 west of Painesville
Wild mid-Victorian jigsaw work and turning.

34. Old South Church (1859)
Romanesque

Chillicothe and Eagle Roads, Kirtland

Organized in 1819, this is one of the oldest congregations in the Western Reserve, and was originally served by Joseph Badger, the Reserve's first itinerant preacher. A possible source for the design is *The Model Architect* (see p. 229).

35. Old South Church. The doorway and windows are capped by hood moldings.

36

37

38

39

40

36. Mormon Temple (1833–36)
Kirtland
The Mormon Temple, one of the Reserve's most precious relics, was begun in 1833 under the leadership of Joseph Smith, Jr., and was dedicated in 1836. Able bodied members of the sect built the 79 foot-long edifice, which has walls two feet thick and woodwork of walnut, beech, basswood, and oak. The box pews accommodate 400 persons. The style is a composite of Federal and Gothic.

37. Mormon Temple. One of the twin doorways.

38. Mormon Temple. Capital of interior column.

39. Mormon Temple. The multiple pulpits at the west end of the interior are repeated at the east end.

40. Mormon Temple. The vestibule contains two symmetrical curved staircases.

41. Henry Earl House (1841)
Classic-Vernacular
Pierson's Knob, Kirtland
Henry Earl, builder
The most delightful element of this simple one-story house is the doorway, with its bold stone Doric columns, lintel, and cornice.

42. Henry Earl House. Doorway.

41

42

43. Robinson-Elwell House (c. 1833)
Classic Revival
3742 Erie Street, Willoughby
Jonathan Goldsmith, builder
This is quite similar to the Mathews house. Here, once again, Goldsmith has used the T-plan.

44. Robinson-Elwell House. The wings are set far back from the facade.

45. Robinson-Elwell House. The front doorway is very similar to that of the Mathews house.

46. Robinson-Elwell House. The house has been converted into apartments, as this rear view indicates. It needs attention badly, but could be restored.

47. 367 River Street
Greek Revival (transitional)
Madison
Talbot Hamlin, in *Greek Revival Architecture in America,* calls attention to the rarity of such transitional works at the end of the Greek Revival and mentions jigsawed cornice brackets and curious columns as a symptom of its sudden decline.

44

48. Paige House (c. 1830)
Greco-Federal
25 East Main Street, Madison
Addison Kimball, builder

The original owner was Judge David R. Paige. The architectural integrity of this splendid early home is compromised by the incongruous doorway. The shallow arcading over the columns is like that at "Brownwood," at Bloomfield in Trumbull County.

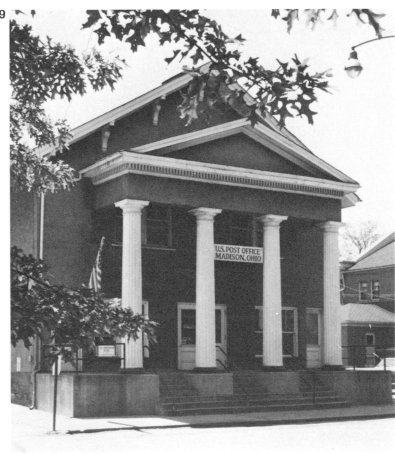

49. Post Office (1867)
Greek Revival (transitional)
Madison
Pancost and Turber, builders

The first town hall of this community. The eaves brackets foreshadow the sudden end of the Greek Revival.

50. 232 River Street
Tuscan
Madison

An interesting application of Tudor drip moldings over the windows of an essentially Tuscan house.

51. "La Riziere"
Classical Revival
Route 84 west of Madison

A good early house, partly hidden by a later porch. The doorway is round-headed.

LAKE COUNTY 89

52. Dr. Winans House (1876)
Victorian
143 River Street, Madison

No more flamboyant expression of high Victorian design or more exuberant use of the lathe and jigsaw can be found in northeastern Ohio.

53. Addison Kimball House (1825)
Vernacular
390 West Main Street, Madison
Addison Kimball, builder

If architecture may be thought of as the assembling of component parts so as to yield a style, this house depends for its architectural character on the style of its doorway. The Kimball family has occupied the house since its construction.

54. Kimball House (1868)
Tuscan
467 West Main Street, Madison

Five generations of Kimballs have
lived here since the land was bought
in 1812 by Addison Kimball. The
broad eaves, with their brackets, and
the rooftop cupola are common
features of the style. The mansard
roof, adopted around this time as
a fashionable form, allowed such
houses to have a complete third story.

55. Kimball House. Entrance.

56. Whipple-VanDyck House (1865)
Greek Revival
1340 East Main Street, Madison

Said to have originally had brackets under its eaves, this house now shows pure Greek Revival lines. It is impressively sited on a rise overlooking the road. The interior has plain, boldly designed woodwork.

57

57. Madison Savings and Loan Company (c. 1875)
Victorian
The Common, Madison

Brick pilasters with white capitals add interest to what would otherwise have been a plain wall surface. The corbeled brickwork, arched window hoods, and eaves brackets heighten the variety and interest.

58. Behm-Oberly House
Vernacular
The Common, Madison

This charming residence gains its distinction from its decorative fretwork. It was long inhabited by members of the Behm family.

58

59. Unionville United Church of Christ
(c. 1840–45)
Greek Revival
Unionville
Donald Barnes, builder

Obviously, the tower of this church suffers from recent remodeling. One can imagine the way it must have been, with pilasters against flush siding like that of the facade.

60

61

60. Old Tavern (1818–20)
Vernacular
Unionville

Mainly built around 1818, this building received its two-story portico in 1820. This site has had an inn on it continuously since 1798, the first being a log cabin.

61. Barnes-Goddard House (c. 1832)
Greek Revival
6860 East Main Street, Unionville
"Mr. Barnes," builder

No one interested in our early architecture could pass this house without admiring the strong corner pilasters, the entablatures, and the decorative detailing of the doorway. Like many of the homes of its time it was built with oak corner posts and girts, with 4 x 4″ studding of softer wood. Clapboards were nailed directly to the studs, and the interior finish was of plaster reinforced with cattle hair. Originally the roof was of shingles. In 1860 the house was acquired by Erastus Goddard and has remained in his family.

62. Connecticut Land Company Office (c. 1817)
Classic Revival
Unionville
Abraham Tappan, builder (?)

Abraham Tappan, said to have been the builder of this handsome little structure, was an important surveyor for the Connecticut Land Company and its successors. The front porch is a most unfortunate later addition, and it is to be doubted that the lean-to wing was part of the original building.

63. Elbridge Warner House (c. 1851)
Route 84 east of Unionville

This brick house, long called "Maplewood Farms," is a curious but impressive mixture of stepped gable ends, blind arcading, Palladian windows, and a Greek Revival doorway. It would be pleasanter if the roof were arranged in the conventional manner. The builder, Elbridge Warner, was the son of Nathan Warner of Hinsdale, Massachusetts, and came to the Reserve when he was one year old.

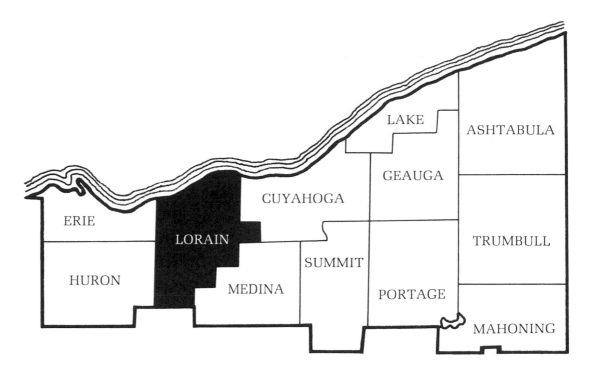

LORAIN COUNTY

Lorain County was erected in 1822 and organized in 1824 from Huron, Medina, and Cuyahoga counties. Elyria, the county seat, was founded and first settled by Heman Ely in 1817.

Oberlin, home of Oberlin College, established in 1833, is famous for the music which it offers, the art which it collects, and the drama which it produces; it has distinguished buildings in a variety of styles. Many of the most interesting Oberlin buildings, such as the Institute of Music buildings and the King Building (Minoru Yamasaki), the Allen Memorial Art Museum and the Divinity School (Cass Gilbert), and the Sophronia Brooks Auditorium (Wallace Harrison) have been built since 1900 and are therefore outside the scope of this volume.

Wellington and environs are recommended for a leisurely look at a prosperous Western Reserve town not greatly changed over the last hundred years. Her well-tended homes have not suffered from the encroachments of industrial expansion, or as yet from sprawling shopping centers. But we advise the reader not to stop with a view of Wellington, as there is much to be seen southward along Route 58 as far as Huntington and west along Route 162 to New London.

Among the architectural treasures in Lorain County are a cluster of stone homes in the Avon-Sheffield vicinity, including the Burrell House at Sheffield and the Hurst-Tomes House at Avon, which in many respects is one of the most remarkable early residences remaining. At Lorain there is the Milton Garfield house, and the Cahoon-Amidon house, immediately east of Elyria, is another Lorain County delight not to be passed over.

The Common, Elyria
Children play on an old cannon

1

1. Town Hall (1885)
Late Victorian
Main Street, Wellington
Oscar Cobb, architect

This picturesque town hall is near the center of Wellington. The date of construction is given on the keystone of the unusual horseshoe window on the third floor. The turrets suggest a medieval castle, and the fancy gables have more or less the form of Gothic ogee arches. Altogether, a Gothic-Moorish composition pleasing to the eye. There is a large gymnasium in a wing to the rear. The architect was a Chicagoan.

2. Wetzel-Fisher House (1865)
Victorian
Route 18, east of Wellington

The delicate fretwork and the columns are of particular interest.

3. Kent Warner House (1868)
Tuscan
South Main Street, Wellington
William Koehl, architect

The Warner house, undoubtedly the most pretentious in town, is an outstanding example of the Tuscan villa of the mid-Victorian period. Inside, on the ground floor, a sitting room and a parlor flank a spacious central hallway.

4. Kent Warner House. Porch. The doorway has been remodeled.

5. Kent Warner House. Mantelpiece in parlor.

2

8

9

6. Couch-Wells House (1849)
Greek Revival
147 South Main Street, Wellington
A. G. Couch, builder (?)
This interesting house was the residence of Albert Couch, a pioneer cabinet maker from Tolland, Massachusetts, who lived here until 1903. The Wells family, who acquired the property in 1909, added the dormers in 1910 and the side porch in 1913. The eared window frames, inside and out, and the "Huntington windows," or doorway sidelights, are notable refinements.

7. "Greenwood Farms"
Greek Revival
Route 18 west of Brighton
The cobblestone foundation is of particular interest.

8. House (c. 1840)
Greek Revival
Route 58 south of Wellington
The difference between this house and some of the suburban houses we build today is all to the advantage of this simple building, with its developed style and attention to detail. The delightful corner pilasters and doorway columns are inspired by builder's handbooks.

9. House, Route 58. Doorway.

11

10. Hurst-Tomes House (1843)
Greek Revival
33065 Detroit Avenue, Avon
William Hurst, builder

In the northeastern part of Lorain County there are a number of stone houses. The most pretentious of these, and the finest stone house in the Western Reserve, is this one, owned first by William Hurst and later by Charles Tomes. The stone is dressed to a smooth surface and laid, in the main body of the house, as coursed ashlar. The contrast with most stonework of the period is remarkable. The doorway, with its rare eared exterior architrave, is particularly handsome. The house still retains its fine kitchen hearth and bake oven. Made for the centuries, this house cost 640 dollars to build.

11. Hurst-Tomes House. Detail of cornice and blocking course.

12. Hurst-Tomes House. East front, showing service wing.

13. Hurst-Tomes House. Archway in service wing.

14

NORTH RIDGEVILLE
CITY HALL

104   LORAIN COUNTY

16

14. Town Hall (c. 1875)
Victorian
North Ridgeville

An example of a type of Victorian public building design not uncommon in the Reserve.

15. Cahoon-Amidon House (c. 1850?)
Tuscan
38369 Center Ridge Road, North Ridgeville

One of the finest examples of the Tuscan villa style is this house, with its paired brackets under the broad eaves and their counterparts in miniature on the porch. A date of 1819 is sometimes given for this house, but the appearance suggests a date no earlier than 1840.

16. Cahoon-Amidon House. Rosette in parlor ceiling.

17. Vair House (1837?)
Tuscan
Third and West Streets, Elyria

If there is construction dating from 1837 in this house, it must have been much remodeled to gain its present Victorian appearance. The porch columns are sandstone monoliths. The interior woodwork is simple but massive.

18. Hart House (c. 1870)
Victorian
525 East College Street, Oberlin

Considered by some the best early house in the town.

19. First Church in Oberlin (1842–43)
Greek Revival
Oberlin

When built, the First Church must have had one of the largest seating capacities in the Reserve. Long used by Oberlin College as an assembly hall, it could accommodate 1,800 persons. Simple in design, it cost only $12,000. The date on the sign indicates that the congregation antedates the building.

20. 58 College Street
Federal
Oberlin

There is a great similarity between this doorway and that of the Nutting house at Hudson. Oberlin was "hacked out of the wilderness" in the early 1830's, and this must have been one of its earliest houses.

21. Milton Garfield House (c. 1839)
Greek Revival
4921 Detroit Road, Lorain

Greek in its overall design, this doorway nevertheless has columns recalling the Federal style.

22. M. B. Rath House (c. 1840)
Greek Revival
4789 Detroit Road, South Lorain

This impressive house is unusual in lacking box cornices, with their horizontal soffits, or any suggestion of a pediment. And most unusual are the raking capitals this arrangement requires. The doorway is highly developed, with a dentiled transom, as are the window architraves, with their corner blocks.

18

19

20

21

22

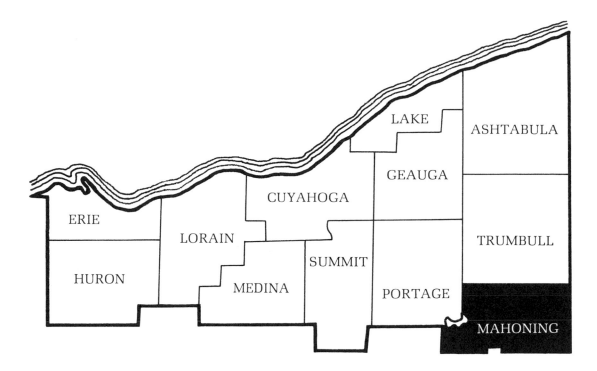

MAHONING COUNTY

Mahoning County was formed from parts of Trumbull and Columbiana
counties in 1846, and the county seat established at Canfield, little more
than two miles north of the Western Reserve base line. (As constituted,
about two-fifths of Mahoning County lies outside the Reserve.)

Visitors will find the towns of Canfield and Poland, in the vicinity of
Youngstown, to be of great interest. The public common, or green, in Canfield is an elongated rectangle with a north-south axis, anchored at the
north end by the handsome Judge Eben Newton House (1826) and at the
other extremity by the arresting white Greek Revival courthouse of 1848.
It is unfortunate that the fine residence and law office of Elisha Whittlesey,
Canfield's most illustrious citizen, originally on or adjacent to this wooded
common, have not been preserved in situ. The latter was removed to a
"pioneer village" on the fairground south of town in the mid 1960's. The
delightful and unique brick office suffers as a result of its detachment from
earlier familiar surroundings, and the town center a lessening of its original
charm. It is unfortunate that Canfield has not been more alert to the value
of its architectural heritage, for what was a decade or two ago one of the
loveliest commons in the entire Reserve is fast being ruined by commercialism. Poland is doing somewhat better; its Main Street is truly one of
the treasure places of the region. From the Public Library, located in a
hollow at the edge of Yellow Creek, one may follow a sylvan trail through
the woods as unspoiled as when Jonathan Fowler, in earlier days, hunted
there to provide for his table. West of Poland, on McKinley Memorial
Highway, stands the old Billius Kirtland house, which deserves a better
fate than the bulldozer.

The architecture hunter, in passing through Youngstown, should pro-
ceed down Wick Avenue, the city's once-prestigious residential thoroughfare, even though many of the fine homes have either been taken over by,
or are giving way to, the expansion of Youngstown State University.
McKim, Mead and White's Butler Art Institute, on the avenue, is a jewel.

Billius Kirtland House (1830)
A plain but handsome Federal house
at Poland

109

1

2

1. Elisha Whittlesey Law Office
Canfield
This tiny brick building was for many years the office of Elisha Whittlesey, who came from Connecticut and became one of Ohio's most distinguished citizens. Originally it faced the lovely town green of Canfield, but it now stands in a "pioneer village" on the fairgrounds. A number of famous lawyers received their training in this building, among them Joshua Giddings and Benjamin Wade.

2. Elisha Whittlesey Law Office. Repairs to the plaster ceiling uncovered a typical Victorian version of fireproof construction: brick vaults turned between iron joists. A fire door of iron separates the office from the entrance vestibule.

3. Judge Eben Newton House (1826)
Federal (transitional)
The Common, Canfield

Of the many fine houses that once surrounded the common, few are left. One of these is the Eben Newton house. The awkward entrance hood and the sun porch are additions. The classical detail seen on the front decorates all sides of the building. The sunburst in the pediment is repeated in the Sturgis-Kennan-Fulstow house of 1834 in Norwalk: more than a coincidence, perhaps, in view of Elisha Whittlesey's part in founding Norwalk. The house is now used as a restaurant.

4. Judge Eben Newton House. The elaborate Federal paneling of the front parlor is a surprise to the visitor.

5

6

5. Ruggles-Coope House (1846)
Greek Revival
17 Court Street, Canfield
Among the most interesting houses in
Canfield is this one, built by Charles
Ruggles in 1846. The coved cornice and
the octagonal columns are most
unusual, although the latter feature
appears also in the Sturgis-Kennan-
Fulstow house at Norwalk.

6. Ruggles-Coope House. Portico.

7. First Mahoning County Courthouse (1848)
Greek Revival
Canfield
This brick adaptation of Greek temple architecture, which served as the courthouse for thirty years, dominates the south end of the town common. It is now used as an office building.

8. First Mahoning County Courthouse. The round-headed doorway is the only non-Grecian ornamental feature of the building's exterior.

9

10

11

12

13

9. Billius Kirtland House (1830)
Federal
1525 McKinley Highway, Poland

In 1800, Turhand Kirtland was given the township of Poland as a reward for his service to the Connecticut Land Company. His son Billius, obviously a man of taste, built this house thirty years later. The doorway is the most interesting feature of a rather plain exterior. The house is now threatened by road construction. Another son of Turhand Kirtland was Jared P. Kirtland, early Western Reserve naturalist.

10. Billius Kirtland House. A rare example, in the Western Reserve, of a curving staircase.

11. Billius Kirtland House. This Federal fireplace, at the end of the center hall, is similar to ones in Asher Benjamin's *American Builder's Companion.*

12. Billius Kirtland House. Compare the parlor woodwork here with that of the Eben Newton house in Canfield.

13. Jonathan Fowler's Old Stone Tavern (1804)
Vernacular
Poland

This primitive gable, with chimneys joined by a parapet, may be the only early one executed in stone in the Reserve. James R. Stewart operated the tavern, under the name of the Sparrow House, between 1840 and 1860.

14. 215 Main Street (c. 1838)
Greek Revival
Poland

The porch, though harmonious, is probably not original. The frieze windows are characteristic of the period of construction.

15

16

15. John Hunter House (c. 1830)
Greek Revival
307 Main Street, Poland
Hunter, a merchant, was the first occupant of this house. In 1894 it was acquired by the Poland Union Seminary for use as a dormitory.

16. Kennedy House (1845)
Greek Revival (modified)
Main Street, Poland
This house was built for a Mr. Liddle, who sold it almost immediately to the Stoddard family. Eventually, it was sold to Judge James B. Kennedy, whose name is now associated with it. Today it serves as the town hall.

17. Kirtland-Hine House (1845)
Greek Revival
441 Main Street, Poland
This fine house was built by George Kirtland, brother of Jared and Billius. The flush siding sets off the fine and beautiful detailing of the entrance. The whole entrance, including the iron porch cresting, is derived from Asher Benjamin's *The Practice of Architecture* (1833) (p. 221).

18. "Seven Gables" (1870)
Carpenter Gothic
32 McKinley Parkway, Poland
An impressive Victorian house.

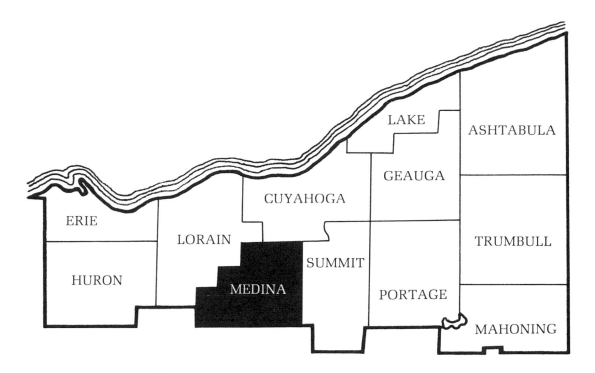

MEDINA COUNTY

Medina County was formed in 1812, but not organized until 1818. Settlement of this region, as indeed all of the land west of the Cuyahoga, was retarded by the War of 1812, during which the British on the western lake shore were a constant threat. Medina, the county seat (at first called Mecca), owes its spacious public square to the generosity of Elijah Boardman, original owner of a large part of Medina township. The earliest settlers lived in log cabins, sometimes for many years, but frame dwellings and barns commenced to be built in 1818–19. The first was a combination home and store in Medina Village, owned by a Mr. Shoals. Not until 1830 did Joseph Harris, the first settler in Medina County (1811), move from a cabin to a large frame house on an Indian mound in the vicinity of Lodi.

While Medina itself has its attractions, the most charming town is Weymouth, a little jewel of a village, nestled in a hollow and happily removed from the vehicular traffic of nearby Route 3.

The homestead of master builder Burritt Blakeslee, about whom I. T. Frary wrote so understandingly in *Early Homes of Ohio,* still stands on Route 70, a short distance west of Route 3. While the outside is quite unchanged, the altered interior is disappointing. With the benefit of an additional third-of-a-century perspective, we may see Burritt Blakeslee as a representative of the many hard-working, solid, honest, capable artisans who came to this frontier land in the first half of the nineteenth century and who, mastering the simple classical forms of the day, built a great deal of the work shown in this volume.

Western Reserve Barn, Route 18
The overlapping boarding makes a
dentil-like shadow pattern on this
otherwise plain structure

119

1. Courthouse (1841, c. 1875)
Victorian
The Common, Medina
T. Dudley Allen, architect
The Medina County courthouse is situated on the east side of one of the lovely town squares of the Reserve. It shows the popularity of French forms at the time of its completion, particularly in its mansard roofs. The cast-iron columns were made by the Younglove Structural Iron Works of Youngstown, and their name appears in the column bases. This Victorian exterior, however, is wrapped around an earlier Greek Revival courthouse, whose exterior is still visible from some angles.

2. The Common
Medina
The Common was a gift of Elijah Boardman, who owned most of the land in the township when Medina was founded in 1818. Shown here is the south side, the "Town Hall and Engine House," with its white trim, and several mid-Victorian store fronts.

3. Weymouth Community Church (1835)
Greek Revival
Weymouth

This choice Greek Revival edifice was built by sixteen families as a Congregational church. Local historians say that the portico, with its fluted Doric columns, and the belfry, which give the church its character, were additions of 1855. As is often the case, flush siding was used on the entrance front and clapboards elsewhere. The square tower, with its recessed columns, is one of the finest in the Reserve. The interior has its original pews. The building has served as a community church since the 1920's, when the Congregationalists found it impossible to maintain it alone.

4. Pierce-Parish House (1846)
Greek Revival
7376 Medina-Norwalk Road

Splendid early homes appear unexpectedly along the country roads; this is such a house. All the signs of the Greek Revival are here, including the pedimental gables and the arrangement of the rather unusually

5

detailed doorway. The foundation is of boulders, and the frame is of 10-inch hand-hewn timbers mortised together and fastened with wooden pegs. The center hallway, with a parlor on either side, has a handsome staircase with a walnut handrail on turned balusters. The interior woodwork is well designed, with the window trim similar in form to the exterior trim of the doorway.

5. Litchfield Congregational Church (1847)
Greek Revival
Litchfield
Another interesting Greek Revival church in Medina County. Here, as at Weymouth, the entrance front has flush siding. It seems likely that the tower was not so austere as it is now; possibly, it was decorated with corner pilasters.

6. Litchfield Congregational Church. Doorway.

7. Episcopal Church (1841)
Greek Revival
Wadsworth
An impressive temple front, despite the rather exaggerated entasis of the unchanneled Doric columns. The belfry is noteworthy. For many years this was a Mennonite church.

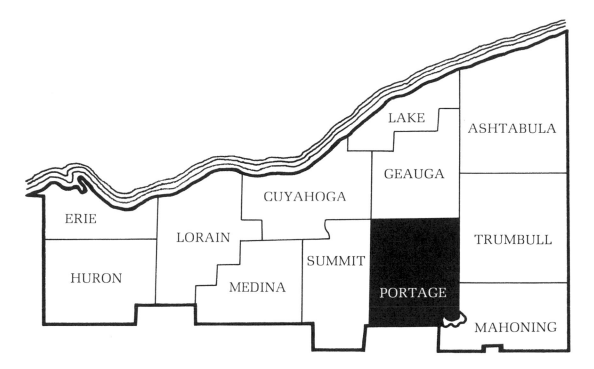

PORTAGE COUNTY

Portage County was erected and organized in 1808 from Trumbull. Its name is derived from the fact that Portage Path, a seven-mile trail over a height of land that formed a link in the passage from Lake Erie to the Ohio River by means of the Cuyahoga and Tuscarawas rivers, traverses it. (Portage Path is now in Summit County, which was formed, in part, from Portage.) At one time the county was nicknamed "Cheesedom" because such great quantities of cheese were produced in Aurora, Bainbridge, Hudson, and other communities.

The county's first settler was Benjamin Tappan of Connecticut, who in 1799 made his way to the vicinity of Ravenna as agent on behalf of his father, Benjamin Tappan, Sr., principal proprietor of the township. The story is told that young Tappan encountered David Hudson, also en route to the Reserve, at Irondequoit, New York, on the shore of Lake Ontario. Hudson, a direct descendant of Henry Hudson, settled in the town which takes his name, which was originally within the limits of Portage County.

The county is dotted with towns deriving their names from the New England communities from which the settlers came: Suffield, Brimfield, New Milford, Deerfield, and Windham. The most rewarding region for an architectural tour is that traversed by state Route 82, and particularly the towns of Aurora, Mantua Center, Hiram, and Mantua. The church at Atwater, in the county's southern part, is one of the most highly regarded in the Reserve. Deerfield gives evidence of having been a delightful place, but unfortunately the interesting structures around its common suffer from inattention and thoughtless commercialism.

Old Brick Tavern, Route 44 at
  Pioneer Trail
Said to have been built in 1825, but
with an obviously Victorian porch

1

126   PORTAGE COUNTY

1. Congregational Church (1841)
Greco-Gothic
Atwater

This has long been considered one of the very finest churches in the Western Reserve. The Gothic windows and the domed cupola are major deviations from the prevailing Greek Revival character of the design. The pairing of the outermost Ionic columns is a device satisfying to the eye and was used, in a more subtle manner, by the ancient Greeks to give an added appearance of stability to their temple fronts.

2. Congregational Church.
Detail of porch.

3. C. R. Howard House (1853)
Gothic
411 East Garfield Street, Aurora
M. Smith, builder

This fine home owes a great deal of its charm to its cobblestone facing. If there are others like it in the Reserve, we are unaware of them. A monumental forcefulness is given the house by the massive lintels and quoins, only to be contradicted by the light, fanciful vergeboard.

4. C. R. Howard House. Doorway.

8

9

5. Emery Root House (c. 1830)
Federal
Route 43 and Chillicothe Road, Aurora
An old abstract records that a
Reverend Seward sold this house in
1830; it then faced the "Pittsburgh
Road," the present Route 43. The
portico must have been added later.
The doorway is the most obviously
Federal detail of the exterior.

6. Emery Root House. Stairway.

7. 84 Chillicothe Road (1878?)
Tuscan Bracketed
Aurora
Charles Harmon, builder
A villa near the center of town in a
style often seen in the Reserve. Interior
remodelings have left little of interest.

8. Chauncey Eggleston House (c. 1820)
Federal
Eggleston Road, Aurora
Chauncey Eggleston, builder
General Eggleston made the brick for
this house from clay dug on the site.
The mortar was made from burned
limestone quarried on the nearby
Ebenezer Sheldon farm. The doorway
gives the house its Federal character.

9. Chauncey Eggleston House.
Doorway.

10

11

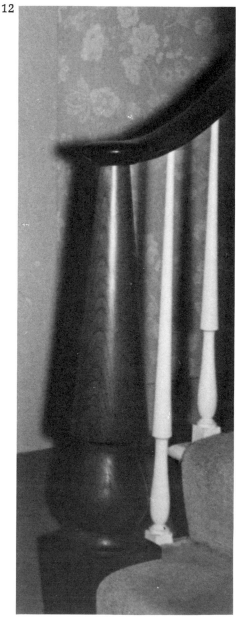

12

10. Store Building
Greek Revival
Route 306 and Chillicothe Road,
Aurora
Without its signs this former
store building would be very handsome
indeed. Obviously, the date 1815
shown here is dubious; the Greek
Revival style is rare in this region
before 1830. The ground floor interior
is of little interest.

11. Ebenezer Sheldon House (1851)
Greek Revival
Pioneer Trail, Aurora Township
This late Greek Revival house has
detailing of considerable refinement.

12. Ebenezer Sheldon House.
Newelpost.

13. Zeno Kent House (c. 1820?)
Greek Revival
Hudson Road, Aurora Township
Zeno Kent came to Aurora in 1806. The
date usually given for this house
seems too early for so mature a Greek
Revival doorway. Unless something
is done for this house soon, it will be
lost.

14. Zeno Kent House. Doorway.

15. Zeno Kent House. Panel of outside
door, late Victorian period.

13

14

15

PORTAGE COUNTY   131

16

17

132　　PORTAGE COUNTY

16. Raymond Carlisle House (1836)
Classic
7521 Hiram-Garretsville Road
Pelatiah Allyn, builder
This house was built for Charles
Raymond in 1836, and remained in his
family for nearly 80 years. The east
wing, in the foreground, originally
had an open storage space for wood on
the ground floor, but was fully
enclosed in the late 1860's.

17. Carlisle House (c. 1840?)
Greek Revival
7295 Hiram-Garretsville Road
This Greek Revival house, which has a
commanding position on a hilltop,
shows how a cornice can be continued
across gable ends to form pediments,
which in this case are heavily
emphasized. The corner pilasters, on
the other hand, are inconspicuous.

18. Town Hall (1836–40)
Greek Revival
Mantua Center
Originally, the first floor of such a
town hall was used for town meetings,
while the second floor housed the
school. Surviving cupolas are rare on
these buildings; most of them have
been destroyed by decay or accident.

19. Town Hall, Mantua Center.
Detail of pediment window.

19

20

21

20. H. J. Sanford House (1885)
Victorian
Auburn Road south of Mantua Center
Daniel Plum, builder

A form seen everywhere in the
Reserve: essentially Tuscan, it has a
dormered mansard roof. The
owner was a prosperous farmer.

21. House (c. 1878)
Victorian
Route 82 east of Mantua Center

Pathetic now, this was also the proud
home of a prosperous farmer. Note
the similarity to the H. J. Sanford
house: a very similar design, translated
into brickwork.

22. Hilltop Christian Church
Mantua

A peculiar combination: a Palladian
window; a Gothic window; and a
cupola of around 1880.

22

PORTAGE COUNTY   135

23. William H. Krafts Block
(after 1870)
Mantua

The cast-iron columns often seen on Victorian store fronts of this size are missing here. The ornamental brickwork above is interesting.

24. H. L. Hine House (c. 1895)
Shingle Style
4624 Prospect Street, Mantua

This fine Shingle Style house is said to be modeled after Sagamore Hill, Theodore Roosevelt's Long Island home. The interior is richly decorated with carved paneling. Each of the numerous ground floor rooms has an individually designed fireplace with a decorative overmantel. The third floor contains a large ballroom. Hine, a local banker, was bankrupted in the panic of 1907.

25. Victorian Stores
Mantua

Typical small-town commercial architecture of the 1890's.

26. I.O.O.F. Block and Adjoining Buildings
Victorian
Ravenna

Few people look up to note the 1846 datestone of the I.O.O.F. facade. The fanciful Victorian ornamentation suggests a remodeling at some later date, possibly in the 1870's.

24

PORTAGE COUNTY   137

27

28

29

138   PORTAGE COUNTY

27. Seymour-Jennings House (c. 1850)
Greek Revival
161 North Chestnut Street, Ravenna
Completed around 1850 "after a general plan taken from some old homes in Massachusetts," this house was first owned by Frederick W. Seymour and was in his family for nearly 90 years. The original woodwork remains, but only one of the original marble fireplaces, that in the dining room. The porch should be two stories high to be really effective and well proportioned. Until their death in a blight a few years ago, the house was surrounded by old elm trees. At one time, too, the windows had green shutters. Seriously threatened by commercial expansion, the future of this house is in doubt.

28. Seymour-Jennings House. Porch.

29. Seymour-Stevens House (c. 1880?)
Victorian
151 Chestnut Street, Ravenna
The interior of this house still contains its rich, heavy walnut trim. But a commercial building is under construction eight feet away, and this house will not last long.

30. George Reed House (c. 1880)
Victorian
229 Riddle Street, Ravenna
This once-proud home is now a boarding house. The window heads and quoins are of cut stone.

31. John Singletary House (1826)
Federal
Streetsboro
A highly attractive and imaginative entrance. This house, long an antique shop, is now in danger.

32. Kondik House (c. 1845?)
Greek Revival
4556 Aurora-Mantua Road
It is an amusing game to try guessing the date of a building like this. If this were early Greek Revival, the entablature and pediment would probably be bolder, and one would expect Doric antae rather than corner boards. The detailing of the entrance pilasters is like that in Asher Benjamin's *Practical House Carpenter* (1830), plate 28, and can also be seen in the Claridon church of 1831. Our guess for this house is around 1845.

33

140   PORTAGE COUNTY

33. Marsha Henry House (c. 1838)
Greek Revival
Hiram

One of the oldest houses in Hiram, this was moved to a hilltop south of the town a few years ago.

34. "Bonney Castle" (after 1830)
Greek Revival
Hiram College, Hiram

Long a famous inn and restaurant, this fine work of the 1830's has been owned by Hiram College for the past decade. Plans are under way to restore the interior and to use the building as an "English house" to commemorate the writers and teachers who have been associated with the college over the years.

35. House (c. 1826)
Federal
Route 224 west of the Common, Deerfield

Here is a neglected gem, falling into decay. The doorway is pure Federal. The ornamentation is characteristic of the period before 1830.

36. House, Route 224. Doorway.

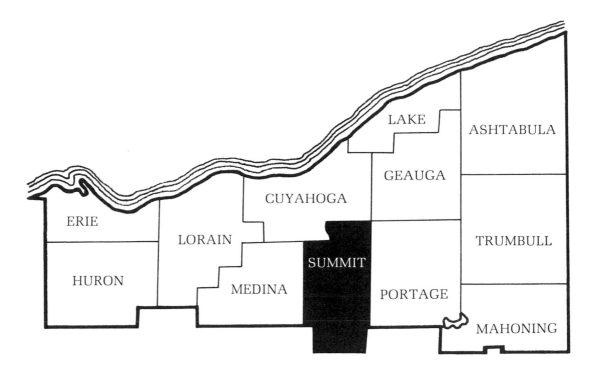

SUMMIT COUNTY

Summit County, formed from Portage, Medina, and Stark Counties in 1840, derives its name from the fact that it was the highest point of land on the Ohio Canal (opened 1827), which traversed it from north to south. The first settlement within the county was made at Hudson, while the area was still in Portage County, by David Hudson in the year 1800. The latter's homestead, built in 1807 and continuously lived in by descendants until 1968, has been restored by Western Reserve Academy. David Hudson envisioned a spiritually motivated, law-abiding community with a college and a church. The church was established by Joseph Badger, the itinerant minister who served numerous early Western Reserve settlements in 1807. Owen Brown, the father of John Brown the abolitionist, settled in Hudson in 1805 and was one of the church's first deacons. The college, Western Reserve College, was founded in 1826, but eventually moved to Cleveland in 1882 to become Western Reserve University. Its buildings, largely erected by Lemuel and Simeon Porter, were then taken over by the "preparatory department," or Academy, which was at first associated with the University but which since 1916 has operated independently as Western Reserve Academy.

Akron, the county seat and most populous city in the county, came into being with the construction of the Ohio Canal in 1825. Simon Perkins is credited with being its founder. He built there in 1832 for his son and namesake the so-called Perkins house, which to this day is Akron's most distinguished historic residence. It is difficult today to find a trace of the canal, which ran through the very heart of the modern city. However, the section between Akron and Peninsula and on toward Cleveland is still largely intact, and there is talk of converting it into a national historic site. Originally a canal and milling town, Akron, in the latter part of the nineteenth century, became the world's largest rubber-maker with the discovery of the vulcanization process and the advent of the automobile. As in Cleveland, the swift development of the city has swept most of the old landmarks aside.

The Common, Twinsburg
(founded 1817)
In the background, the Congregational church

143

1

Tallmadge, today virtually a suburb of Akron, is named for its founder, Benjamin Tallmadge, who interestingly enough came from Litchfield, Connecticut, as did many of the other residents. This may serve to explain the similarity of the Tallmadge church with the slightly later one at Litchfield. It is not unnatural that the settlers of New Connecticut should have desired a church as fine as, and along the lines of, the ones which they had known.

Much that is architecturally interesting in Summit County can be seen and enjoyed by taking Route 91 southward from Twinsburg through Hudson, Stow, and Tallmadge, thence to Akron, and via Portage Path and the West Canal Road to Peninsula, Boston, and Richfield. In the vicinity of Everett, south of Peninsula, one must detour to the Jonathan Hale Homestead (operated by the Western Reserve Historical Society), which is not only an outstanding piece of early architecture, but a fine museum shedding much light on the early life of the settlers. Several structures, including the Benjamin Wade law office, have been relocated here in a "pioneer village."

1. Chapel, Western Reserve Academy (1836)
Greek Revival
Hudson
Lemuel and Simeon Porter, architects

This, without doubt, is the most important work of architecture in a town rich in good architecture. The arcading of the side walls, pleasing in itself, is an incongruity. The tower had a third cubical element, with a flagpole, until around 1870. The brick was made locally. The college library was originally on the ground floor, and a single staircase (replaced by a double one in 1872) led to the chapel itself on the second floor. In 1938 the building was lengthened by two bays, and in 1965 the building was reinforced with a steel skeleton.

2. Chapel, Western Reserve Academy. Interior.

3. President's House, Western Reserve Academy (1828)
Federal
Hudson

Aside from the Congregational church at Tallmadge, this is the most important remaining design of Lemuel Porter, father of Simeon Porter. It was originally built as a residence for professors.

4. President's House. The twin doorways.

5

6

5. Nutting-Bliss House (1831)
Federal
79 Hudson Street, Hudson
Simeon Porter, architect (?)

The residence of Professor Rufus Nutting was restored in 1966. For many years this was the dining hall of Western Reserve College. Today only the exterior is original. The delightful and unusual recessed doorway gives the house its Federal character.

6. Nutting-Bliss House. Doorway.

7. The Athenaeum, Western Reserve
Academy (1843)
Classic Revival
Hudson
Simeon Porter, architect

As in the college chapel, a blind
arcade is used to decorate this facade,
which was once a side wall.
Originally the building had a cupola at
one end and was only three stories
high. The first floor had laboratories
and a prayer room; the second had
a museum room with a coved ceiling.
After a fire in 1916, a fourth story
was added and the building converted
into a dormitory.

8. Seymour House (1841)
Greek Revival
15 Prospect Street, Hudson
Simeon Porter, architect

Many people consider this house,
built for Professor Nathan Seymour,
to be the handsomest in Hudson.
The doorway is a splendid Greek
Revival design. Note the floor-length,
24-light ground floor windows.

11

9. David Hudson House (1807)
Vernacular
Route 91 opposite Western Reserve
Academy, Hudson
This was the most ambitious building
of its date in the Reserve. Still in
the Hudson family in 1968, it is now
the property of Western Reserve
Academy and has been restored to
serve as a faculty residence.

10. David Hudson House. Doorway.

11. Hayden Hall, Western Reserve
Academy (1870, c. 1910)
Hudson
*J. W. C. Corbusier, architect for
conversion*
Built as a cheese warehouse, this
building was later converted into a
community club. At that time the front
was recessed and the Greek
Revival-looking columns added.

14

12. Observatory, Western Reserve Academy (1838)
Hudson
Simeon Porter, architect
This, the second oldest observatory in the United States, was built after the specifications of Professor Elias Loomis, who had visited observatories in England and France. Only the Williams College observatory is older, and that by only three months. The dome rotates on wooden balls running in a track, and the stone telescope mounts extend six feet into the ground.

13. Congregational Church (1865)
Gothic Revival
Hudson
Simeon Porter, architect
During his partnership with Charles W. Heard, 1849–59, Porter learned to use Gothic and Romanesque forms. This doorway is an example of his later work. This building has one curious feature: the spire was built inside the tower and hoisted into place.

14. Farwell House (after 1830, c. 1865?)
Hudson
A curious architectural hybrid: Ionic pilasters with a porch, cornice, and cupola that are pure Victorian bracketed. Local historians say that the fireplaces and other interior woodwork suggest the 1830's.

15

16

15. Brewster House ("The Elms")
(c. 1855)
Gothic Revival
The Common, Hudson
Simeon Porter, architect
A fanciful Gothic experiment in
sandstone, built for a local merchant.
Originally there was a flat-roofed
porch with a bracketed cornice on
either side of the entrance.

16. Beebe House (c. 1853)
Greek Revival
Hudson
Except for the incongruous arched
doorway, this is a late example of the
Greek Revival. It now serves as the
parish house of an Episcopal church.

18

17. The Common
Hudson
An old-fashioned Western Reserve
town common, showing the late
Victorian Ellsworth Tower and the
former Brewster store, now a bank.

18. Street in Hudson
In the foreground, the Ellsworth store
of 1841; in the background, the
Frederick Baldwin house of c. 1832.

19. First Congregational Church (1848)
Greek Revival
Twinsburg
Simeon Porter, architect

One of the most attractive small Greek Revival churches in the Western Reserve. Its details are pure Greek Revival, except for the tower, which seems to the author to be a little too slender to be pure in style. The spire, of course, has no ancient Greek precedent in any case.

20. First Congregational Church. Entrance.

21. First Congregational Church. Interior.

22. Hill-Burridge House (c. 1830)
Greek Revival
9886 Ravenna Road, Twinsburg
James Hill, the first owner, was a bachelor who lived alone in eighteen rooms filled with fine imported furnishings. Now used as a boarding house, its continued existence is precarious.

23. McFarlane-Reed House (c. 1845)
Greek Revival
9869 Ravenna Road, Twinsburg
Harvey McFarlane, a merchant, was the first owner of this house, which was later the property of Elijah Reed. Its most conspicuous feature is the recessed porch. A house of the late Greek Revival.

24. Jonathan Herrick House (1845)
Greek Revival
8327 Twinsburg-Hudson Road
No one with an eye for our early architecture could ignore this splendid stone specimen, or fail to notice the "J.E.H. 1845" on its datestone. Herrick, a township trustee, lived here until his death in 1898. This is perhaps the finest Western Reserve stone house of its period east of the Cuyahoga.

25. Jonathan Herrick House. Doorway.

SUMMIT COUNTY   155

26

27

26. First Congregational Church (1825)
Federal
The Green, Tallmadge
Lemuel Porter, builder

This is one of the most important monuments of the Western Reserve. Its style is still in many ways that of the eighteenth century, although its detailing is Federal. It is interesting to compare it with the Congregational church in Litchfield, Connecticut, built around the same time (p. 212).

27. First Congregational Church. Portico.

28. First Congregational Church. Tower.

SUMMIT COUNTY   157

29

30

29. Col. Simon Perkins House (1837)
Greek Revival
550 Copley Road, Akron
Isaac Ladd, builder (?)
Colonel Perkins was the son of
General Simon Perkins of Warren, the
founder of Akron and the person
largely responsible for bringing the
Ohio Canal through the town. The
similarity of this house to that built
by Isaac Ladd for Frederick Kinsman
at Warren suggests Ladd as the
builder of this one as well: this
particular style is nowhere else to be
found in the Western Reserve. The
site and the stonework, however,
make this a more impressive house
than the one at Warren.

30. Col. Simon Perkins House.
Doorway.

31. Col. Simon Perkins House.
Hallway.

32. Col. Simon Perkins House.
An upstairs bedroom.

33

33. Hower-Crawford House (1869–71)
Victorian
60 Fir Hill, Akron
John H. Hower, designer
This is the best preserved and one of
the most pretentious Victorian houses
in northeast Ohio. Hower, its designer
and first owner, was a successful
Akron industrialist; the house has
remained in his family. It is located
on a height of land east of the city,
a site that enhances the picturesque
character of its overall composition,
its mansard roofs, dormers, and
bracketed eaves.

34. Hower-Crawford House. Front
hall, inside. Note the beautifully
etched door and overdoor panels.

35. Hower-Crawford House. The main
stair rises four stories to the
observation tower.

36. Hower-Crawford House. Beyond
the staircase is a central octagonal hall
leading to all the other rooms of the
ground floor. The door frames are of
walnut from Hower's property.

37. Hower-Crawford House. A parlor.
Note the ceiling rosette.

34

35

36

37

SUMMIT COUNTY   161

38

39

162 SUMMIT COUNTY

40

38. Old Stone Schoolhouse (1840)
Vernacular
Buchtel Street and Broadway, Akron
The oldest surviving schoolhouse in
the city is now used as a museum of
early education in the Western
Reserve.

39. Bronson Memorial Church (1839)
Greco-Gothic
Peninsula
A short distance north of the Hale
Homestead is the early canal town
of Peninsula. This church was built
with a gift of $1,000 from one Herman
Bronson. The entire interior, including
a coved ceiling, was covered with
unpainted wood. The building is only
36 feet long by 24 feet wide, and
seats 98.

40. Newton-Minstry House (1819–20)
Federal
West Richfield
Orson Oviatt, builder
A handsome doorway with an unusual
fan motif.

41

42

44

41. Jonathan Hale Homestead (1826)
Federal
Oak Hill Road, Bath Township
Jonathan Hale, builder

The Hale Homestead was acquired by the Western Reserve Historical Society in 1957, and is open to the public as a museum of early Western Reserve architecture and country life. It is a simple version of Federal architecture in the newly reclaimed wilderness. Jonathan Hale came from Connecticut, and settled in Bath Township in 1810. After building himself a kiln for bricks and lime, which he made from material found on the property, he was able to build himself one of the earliest brick houses in the Cuyahoga valley. A carpenter-joiner from Sandisfield, Massachusetts, John Bosworth, helped lay the brick and did much of the interior woodwork.

42. Jonathan Hale Homestead. The fall of land allows the basement kitchen to have above ground windows. This was the original kitchen hearth.

43. Jonathan Hale Homestead. Another view of the kitchen, showing a replica of another kitchen fireplace.

44. Jonathan Hale Homestead. The first floor parlor contains this finely fluted mantelpiece.

45. Jonathan Hale Homestead. "Pioneer Village," close to the main house, contains several examples of early Western Reserve architecture. A Greek Revival house can be seen to the left, and an early saltbox house to the right.

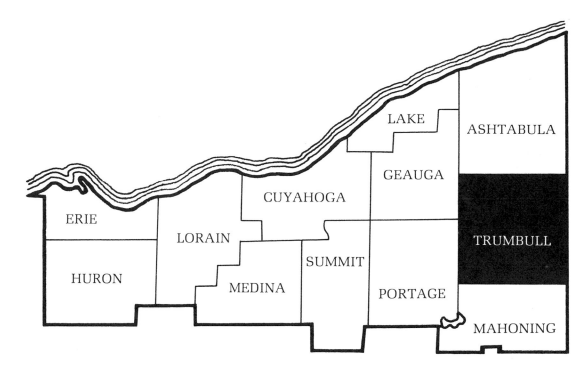

45

TRUMBULL COUNTY

The early history of Trumbull County and its seat Warren is neatly summarized on a bronze plaque affixed to the courthouse which reads as follows:

Warren, the Capital of the Western Reserve

July 10, 1800, Arthur St. Clair, Governor of the Northwest Territory erected the entire Western Reserve as Trumbull County with the seat of justice at Warren. Settlement had been made by Ephraim Quimby and Richard Storer, April 17, 1799.

From the Connecticut Land Company, Ephraim Quimby acquired the land on both sides of the Mahoning River on which Warren now stands and on December 10, 1800, donated this park to the public.

The first court of quarter sessions of Trumbull County convened August 25, 1800, at the residence of Ephraim Quimby near the southwest corner of Main and South Streets. At this meeting the portion of Trumbull County lying East of the Cuyahoga River was divided into eight Civil townships. etc.

Although Warren proper still contains a number of early structures of architectural interest, the southern portion of the county, particularly the corridor between it and Youngstown, has been transformed by industrialization and land developments. For one interested in historic architecture, the most rewarding towns are those in the county's northern part along state Route 87: Mesopotamia, North Bloomfield, Gustavus, and Kinsman. Newton Falls is noted for its covered bridge with accompanying pedestrian walkway.

National McKinley Birthplace
Memorial, Niles
McKinley was born in Niles on
January 29, 1843

1

2

3

1. Peter Allen House. Doorway and window frame. As usual, flush siding is used to make a neutral background to the ornamental work.

2. Peter Allen House (1821)
Federal
State Road, Kinsman
Willie Smith, builder

The Allen house is the masterpiece of early architecture in Trumbull County. It is not surpassed in refinement of detail by any other house in the Western Reserve. That this is so is in large part due to the efforts of its present owner, Alice Logan Blaemire, who managed to have the parlor woodwork, which had been removed to another place around the turn of the century, returned to the house. While the effect of the exterior suggests the Greek Revival temple-fronted house, the detailing— the doorway, the window frames, the pilasters, the entablature, and the pediment light—is Federal.

3. Peter Allen House. The rich upper detailing of the facade.

4

5

6

7

4. Peter Allen House. In no other Federal home of the Western Reserve is the window framing so elaborately and richly treated. The design of the ceiling cornice is probably from Plate 26, Design B of Asher Benjamin's *American Builder's Companion* (1816).

5. Peter Allen House. Hallway.

6. Peter Allen House. The fine mantelpiece in the parlor. Note the similarity in design between the entablature here and that of the front doorway.

7. House (after 1830)
Greek Revival
Kinsman Center

A monumental treatment of a small house. Note the split porch columns at the left and the large sashes, of 12 lights each, in the windows at the right.

170   TRUMBULL COUNTY

8. Presbyterian Church (c. 1832)
Greco-Gothic
Kinsman
Willie Smith, builder
A curious blend of Gothic and
classical forms, but not to be dismissed
without a lingering look.

9. Ephraim Brown House
("Brownwood") (1816)
Federal
Bloomfield
"Brownwood" ranks high in any
listing of Western Reserve landmarks.
It has a fine setting, well back from
the highway. The doorway, the
pilasters, the blind arcading, and the
elliptical pediment light all bear the
mark of the Federal style. On the
other hand, the parlor looks as if time
there had stopped at 1870. The house
is still in the Brown family.

10. House on Route 87
Federal
Bloomfield
This, a mirror image of the central part
of "Brownwood," is just across the
road. Supposedly built by Ephraim
Brown for a niece, it was lived in for
many years by "Uncle Joe" Cook,
manager of Brownwood Farms. Now
a tavern, it has an uncertain future.

11. Wing-McAdoo-Kennedy House
(c. 1846)
Gothic Revival
Bloomfield

Across the road, once again, from "Brownwood," this house was supposedly built for a daughter of Ephraim Brown who married a man named Wing. The Tudor ornament of the windows and dormers is especially delightful. The walls throughout are made of heavy planking. Inside, the best preserved room is the parlor to the left of the entrance. The house was an important "underground railroad" stop and contains hiding places.

12. Schoolhouse
Greek Revival
Route 45 north of Bloomfield Center

Obviously, there was also a window to the right of the doorway. The building was enlarged and converted into an apartment house around 1925.

13. Town Hall (c. 1870?)
Gustavus

A curious building, with a hip roof and a modified mansard tower.

14. Frederick Kinsman House (1832)
Greek Revival
303 Mahoning Avenue, Warren
Isaac Ladd, designer

The land for this impressive house was a wedding gift from General Simon Perkins, whose daughter Olive married Kinsman. The scale of the portico is quite unusual in the Reserve. Two parlors, a sitting room, and a dining room occupied the ground floor, and there were four bedrooms upstairs. Some demolition and addition took place before 1860. The building is presently an annex to the Trumbull County courthouse.

12

TRUMBULL COUNTY   173

16

15. King-Smith House
(after 1820?; after 1850?)
Bracketed
241 Mahoning Avenue NW, Warren
Isaac Ladd, builder (?)

Judging from appearances, this is a Federal house that was modernized in the 1850's. The doorway, the front hall interior, and the flush siding all point to an early date of construction. The aluminum siding and the replacement of the original Ionic porch posts with modern ones have since destroyed the remaining Federal character of the exterior.

16. King-Smith House. Hallway.

18

17. John Stark Edwards House (1807)
Vernacular
Warren

If the building date is indeed 1807, this is possibly the oldest existing house in the Western Reserve. Edwards, a Yale graduate, was the Reserve's first resident attorney and its first representative in Congress.

18. Connecticut Land Company Office (after 1820)
Greek Revival
Warren

Simon Perkins worked in this building as land agent for the Erie Company, a subsidiary of the Connecticut Land Company. Here, too, his son-in-law Frederick Kinsman conducted his business. This is possibly the oldest office building in the Western Reserve. The side wing is modern.

176   TRUMBULL COUNTY

19. Trumbull County Courthouse (1895)
Romanesque Revival
Warren
LaBelle and French, architects
This is the third courthouse to occupy this site. The first, erected in 1815, was replaced by another in 1854, which burned in 1895. The present building uses the Romanesque forms popularized by H. H. Richardson two decades earlier. It is built of local sandstone. The contractor's bid was a little over $140,000.

20. Trumbull County Courthouse. Detail of central element.

21. Log Schoolhouse
The Common, Warren

Doubtless, the oldest schoolhouse in the Reserve. It is more primitive even than the Garfield cabin, as reconstructed at Mentor, in that in this case the logs are untrimmed. On the other hand, the Garfield chimney is of logs, not stone.

22. Methodist Church. The unusually detailed doorway is the handsomest element of the design.

23. Methodist Church (1838)
Greek Revival
Southington

Greek Revival in spirit, but lacking the usual corner pilasters on either the main body of the church or the tower.

TRUMBULL COUNTY   179

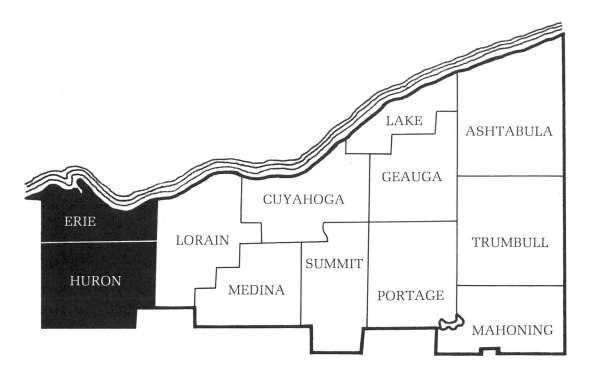

THE FIRELANDS
HURON AND ERIE COUNTIES

As has been mentioned in the historical introduction, the citizens of certain towns in Connecticut, particularly ones along the coast, suffered terrible pillage and burning at the hands of the British between 1777 and 1781. The first to be destroyed, Danbury, may well have been considered a military target because of the large stores of flour, pork, beef, rum, and tents amassed there for the Continental army. However, the destruction inflicted upon the citizens of New London, Groton, New Haven, Fairfield, Norwalk, Greenwich, and Ridgefield was purely the result of terroristic harassment.

An appeal by the citizens of these communities, who believed themselves to have undergone extraordinary hardship, led the General Assembly of Connecticut in 1792 to set aside the westernmost twenty-five miles of the Reserve for the benefit of the "sufferers" and their heirs in perpetuity. However, since claim to this land was not finally relinquished by most of the Indians until 1806, a quarter of a century after the hardships were endured, settlement was retarded until 1809, when surveyor Almon Ruggles was awarded the contract to lay the tract out into five mile-square townships. The initial trickle of settlers was brought virtually to a halt by the War of 1812, so that the real settlement of the Firelands took place after 1815. The entire 500,000-acre tract which was erected in 1809 and organized in 1815 was initially known as Huron County. Erie County was not a separate entity until 1838, when it was erected and organized from Huron and Sandusky counties. Many towns in the Firelands derive their names from their pillaged namesakes in the East.

From the standpoint of architectural interest the two pearls of the region are the towns of Norwalk and Milan. Of all the Firelands communities, none is more delightful or richer in early architecture than Milan, which is best known as the birthplace of Thomas Edison. The quiet character of the present-day town gives little evidence of the commercial activity of the years after the completion in 1839 of the Milan Canal, which linked the

Vredenburgh-Gardiner House
(before 1840)
Set on a grassy, gently rising knoll
among fine old trees

1. Wooster-Boalt-Overhuls House
(c. 1848)
Greek Revival
114 West Main Street, Norwalk

Among the fine homes on West Main Street is this stately house. Originally a young ladies' seminary, it was bought in 1858 by H. M. Wooster. The large doorway and the giant Ionic columns in antis give a monumental quality to this splendidly proportioned front. The porch at the right is almost certainly a later addition.

2. Sturgis-Kennan-Fulstow House
(1834)
Classic Revival
99 West Main Street, Norwalk
William Gale Meade, architect

Another of Norwalk's treasured homes is this one built for Thaddeus Sturgis. It is one of the few in the Reserve to have a two-story portico, and, except for the Ruggles-Coope house at Canfield, it is unique in having octagonal columns. The sunburst pattern on the pediment may have been copied from the Eben Newton house, also at Canfield.

3. Vredenburgh-Gardiner House
(before 1840)
Greek Revival (transitional)
133 West Main Street, Norwalk

This house has a marvelous setting, several hundred feet back from the road. The doorway is Greek Revival, but the large second floor window and the roof balustrade are Federal. Other portions of the house have undergone alteration, but the front remains as built.

inland agricultural areas with lines of communication to the markets of the East. Canal traffic, boat building, milling, and manufactures created the brief prosperity that gave Milan so many fine old houses. There are other exciting and delightful examples of our early architecture in Monroeville, North Fairfield, Berlin Heights, Florence, and Birmingham. The traveller to these will be enchanted too with the charms of Peru and Fitchville, and the many isolated examples of period architecture to be found in unlikely places. The exhibits and the library facilities at the Firelands Museum in Norwalk ought not be overlooked.

3

4

4. Samuel Preston House
(Firelands Museum) (1835)
Greek Revival
Norwalk

This rather unusual house, originally on West Main Street in the center of Norwalk, was built for Samuel Preston, editor of the *Norwalk Reflector*. Half of the upstairs was given over to printing and publishing. The front is essentially classical; if the second floor porch were removed, and Doric or Ionic columns substituted for the square posts, a stately Greek Revival temple front would be the result. The first and second floors are now filled with displays of early life in the Firelands, while the basement houses a valuable library, including several builder's guides.

5

6

7

8

184   THE FIRELANDS—HURON COUNTY

5. Kimball-Wooster-Carpenter House (1833–35)
Federal
54 West Main Street, Norwalk
One of the most careful and exciting restorations ever undertaken in the Western Reserve has made this its finest existing example of a town house in the Federal style. Paul Carpenter, a Norwalk lawyer, brought this house back to its original condition after it had been a run-down tenement.

6. Kimball-Wooster-Carpenter House. In restoring the porch, the old hand-carved capitals were saved. The original columns were made from solid logs, but had to be replaced.

7. Kimball-Wooster-Carpenter House. The east wall; note the elliptical attic light and the parapet gable.

8. Kimball-Wooster-Carpenter House. The attenuated Ionic columns, with their entasis, the swelling entablature, and the leaded overdoor light of this entrance are all typically Federal.

9. Kimball-Wooster-Carpenter House. Detail, showing the unique cornice and the Flemish brickwork bond.

10. Kimball-Wooster-Carpenter House. Stair under restoration.

11. Kimball-Wooster-Carpenter House. The dining room mantelpiece and that of the parlor are identical; this is that of the dining room. Similar designs can be found in Asher Benjamin's *American Builder's Companion.*

12. 161 West Main Street (c. 1857)
Greek Revival (transitional)
Norwalk

The doorway of this beautifully maintained house is a splendid Greek Revival composition. The roof, with its balustraded deck, suggests the incoming Tuscan mode. In the fully developed Tuscan style, the eaves would be flaring, with brackets beneath them, and in the place of the deck there would be a cupola.

13. Martin Hestor House (c. 1833)
Transitional
Ridge Road, five miles south of Norwalk

This venerable brick house, standing alone in the country, is quite similar in style to the Kimball-Wooster-Carpenter house in Norwalk, and may have been built by the same contractor.

14. Brown-Simmons-Schug House (c. 1820)
Greek Revival
The Common, Monroeville

One of the architectural gems of the Western Reserve. It is astonishing to see such a fine expression of the Greek mode, almost at the western edge of the Reserve, at such an early date. The decorative frieze grilles, characteristic of the period, are rare today. Note the wing to the right, with its porch.

15. North Monroeville Congregational Church
Greek Revival
North Monroeville

A small treasure with rare triple-sash windows of 21 lights each.

THE FIRELANDS—HURON COUNTY   187

16. Hosford-Menard House (1856)
Route 20, Monroeville
John Hosford, builder

This is the finest remaining octagon house in the Western Reserve. It has quadrilateral rooms on both floors, surrounding a circular stair which rises to the cupola. The left-over spaces form storage closets. The brickwork is laid in a variant of Flemish bond.

17. Hosford-Menard House.
The veranda.

19

18. Drake Funeral Home (after 1835?)
Main and Hollister Streets,
Monroeville

A curious building, with a Federal
doorway and a bracketed cornice of
the middle of the nineteenth century.

19. Drake Funeral Home. Doorway.

20

21

20. Hoyt's Department Store (1882)
Victorian
North Fairfield

In the early days of the Firelands,
North Fairfield was a trade rival of
Norwalk. Deprived of railroad service,
its importance declined, but it has
kept a number of interesting old
buildings. This Victorian store,
dominating the town center, is one of
them. The Corinthian cast iron
columns made possible a large window
area for the store front.

21. Hoyt's Department Store.
Ground floor.

23

22. Judge Reed House (after 1850)
Gothic Revival
North Fairfield
Sackville West, builder
This house gains its character from its eaves brackets, its stone lintels, and its doorway which, though essentially Greek Revival, has lancet-headed sidelights. It used to have a porch, but this was removed in 1935. The walls are nine inches thick, and the roof timbers are hand-hewn and pegged in place.

23. Judge Reed House. Doorway.

24

25

192   THE FIRELANDS—HURON COUNTY

24. Rolley House (1840)
Greek Revival
North Fairfield
Scott and Alcott Rolley, builders

This sturdy brick house, whose
datestone, in the pediment, gives its
age, needs careful maintenance
if it is to survive.

25. L. A. Selyem House (1825?)
Greek Revival
Route 162, Fitchville
"Lize" Palmer, builder

The recessed porch is an unusual
feature of this house. The
well-developed Greek Revival forms
make the accepted date for this house
of 1825 suspicious. The house is
supposed to have been a stop on the
"underground railroad."

26. Methodist Church
Peru

This church, abandoned and with
many windows broken, stands at the
northern edge of the town. The
brickwork bond, a variant of Flemish
bond, makes a strong wall pattern.

27

28

27. Kelley Block (c. 1869)
Victorian
The Common, Milan

Long admired by architectural historians, this "block" of stores dominates the eastern side of the town common. The division of the second floor by pilasters, the curving of the cornice to suggest a pediment, and especially the cast-iron arcade of the ground floor give this building its interest. This building serves its purpose as well today as when it was erected.

28. Kelley Block.
The ground floor arcade.

29. Police Station (1886)
Victorian
Milan

A tiny building, but with a mansard roof and a single Baroque dormer.

30. Edison Birthplace (1842)
Greek Revival
Edison Drive, Milan

Samuel Edison, father of the inventor, came to Milan in 1839. He built this house in 1842, on the edge of the ravine through which the Milan Canal and the Huron River run, and here in 1847 Thomas Edison was born. The house is maintained as a museum by the Edison Birthplace Association.

THE FIRELANDS—ERIE COUNTY   195

31

31. Mitchell-Turner House (1848)
Greek Revival
128 Center Street, Milan
Zenas King, builder
Next to Edison's birthplace, this is
Milan's best-known house. Zenas King,
at the time when he built the house,
was also engaged in experiments for
testing the strength of cast iron
structural members that led to the use
of this material in bridge construction.

32. Mitchell-Turner House.
View of portico.

32

33. Mitchell-Turner House.
Note the unusual capitals and
pediment sculpture.

34. Mitchell-Turner House. The
exquisite doorway, derived from a
design by Minard Lafever in *The
Beauties of Modern Architecture*
(p. 222).

35

36

35. Cherry-Lockwood-Moore House
(1835–36)
Greek Revival (transitional)
West Front Street, Milan
Nathan Jenkins, builder

The front of this house is most
impressive, despite the peculiar
spacing of the giant Ionic columns.

36. Cherry-Lockwood-Moore House.
The doorway has a pronounced
Federal character still, and may be
modeled after that of the Kimball-
Wooster-Carpenter house in Norwalk.

38

37. J. C. Lockwood House (1851, 1880)
Victorian
30 Edison Drive, Milan

One of the most pretentious Victorian houses of the Western Reserve. As originally built, it was a fine Tuscan house of two floors. The addition of the tower, mansard roof, and other elements made the house not only larger but more picturesque. The interior is spacious, with openings framed with heavy wooden trim, but is not as interesting as one might anticipate.

38. Hamilton-Rodman House (1828)
Greek Revival (transitional)
Milan

Considered by many to be the finest doorway in the town.

39

39. Roft House (1858?)
Tuscan
914 West Perkins Avenue, Sandusky
A fine example of the Tuscan style which filled the void left by the departure of the Greek Revival. The flaring, bracketed eaves and central cupola are characteristic.

40. Oran Follet House (1837)
Greek Revival
404 Wayne Street, Sandusky
The Follet house is a very important architectural landmark, and an amazingly sophisticated design for this early date in the western Firelands. The porch and entrance are unsurpassed in beauty anywhere in the Western Reserve. The south wall is unusual, in that it has no openings either on the first or second floors. Oran Follet was the editor of the *Ohio State Journal.*

41. Oran Follet House. The porch, with its double flight of steps.

42. Oran Follet House. Doorway.

THE FIRELANDS—ERIE COUNTY   201

43

44

43. Butler-Carlson-Bettcher House
(1827)
Classic Revival
Birmingham

An early brick town house of Federal type. The gable has a lovely elliptical light with a vertical long axis. The doorway is Greek Revival.

44. Butler-Carlson-Bettcher House. The parlor woodwork is simple Greek Revival design. The interior shutters fold into the splayed sides of the skillfully executed window casings.

45. Firelands Community Bank (1897)
Romanesque Revival
Berlin Heights

An eclectic building, combining Romanesque arches and pillars with classical pediments.

46. Town Hall (c. 1850)
Florence

A unique octagonal stone building, used originally as a school.

204   THE FIRELANDS—ERIE COUNTY

47. First Congregational Church
(c. 1840)
Greek Revival
Florence

A fine example of the Greek Revival churches which dot the landscape of the Western Reserve. All the elements are in balance, and all have traditional forms.

48. Presbyterian Church (1848?)
Greek Revival
Huron

The octagonal tower and spire are out of keeping with the temple-fronted church, but the ensemble is still most attractive.

THE FIRELANDS—ERIE COUNTY 205

49

49. Sprigg-Garrett-Hahn House
(c. 1845)
Greek Revival
Bogart Road, west of Huron
With the asphalt facing simulating brick removed, this would be among the finest Greek Revival works in Erie County. It is said to have been owned originally by a General Sprigg of the United States Army.

WESTERN
RESERVE ARCHITECTURE
AND ITS HISTORIC
BACKGROUND

THE CLASSIC REVIVAL

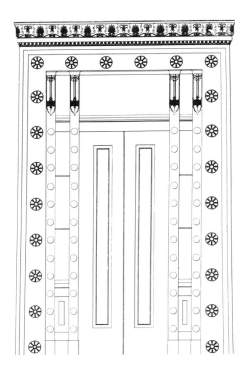

The settlement of the Western Reserve, as we have seen, began for all practical purposes around 1800. Conditions in the Reserve, at that time still a wilderness, were primitive, and for most settlers the first home was a solitary cabin, much like President Garfield's birthplace (p. 70), which is exhibited in replica at "Lawnfield" in Mentor. By 1820, however, the original trickle of incoming settlers had increased to a torrent. Most of these settlers, of course, came from Connecticut, but there were settlers also from other New England states, some of whom had settled briefly in upstate New York. By 1820 many of the present-day communities of the Reserve had been founded, and the general prosperity from farming and trading made it possible for the settlers to build simple frame houses in the styles prevalent in the East. At this time the Roman and free classical forms of the Federal style were yielding to those of the Greek Revival. Both these styles of architecture made their imprint on the building of the Western Reserve, and we therefore begin with an examination of their origins and development.

THE GEORGIAN COLONIAL PERIOD (1720–80)

Naturally, terminal dates are arbitrary; no style displays its new characteristics suddenly on a given date or vanishes on another. The House of Burgesses and the Governor's Palace at Williamsburg, built in the reign of Queen Anne, are in some ways "Georgian," while decidedly Colonial forms appear still during the Federal period. Transitional phases of at least a decade are the rule.

Georgian Colonial forms are borrowings from similar, but usually grander, English prototypes, particularly the designs of Sir Christopher Wren (1631–1723) and James Gibbs (1683–1754). Gibbs was the more influential of the two; his designs for St. Martins-in-the-Fields in London were the models for many Colonial and Federal churches, their towers especially. More importantly, Gibbs' *Book of Architecture* of 1728 was a guide to the gentleman-architects and builders of houses in the colonies. Batty Langley's *City and Country Builder's and Workman's Treasury of Design,* a British work with more than 400 plates, was even more influential than the Gibbs book. Imported architectural guides, indeed, were of immense importance in both this and the succeeding periods until the early nineteenth century, when the guides of Asher Benjamin, Minard Lafever, Edward Shaw, and others made American designs available.

The fully developed Georgian Colonial style varied in form and ornamentation according to the region in which it was used: what was suitable for a New England merchant was not for a southern planter. In general, though, a late Colonial house of some pretensions would have some or all of the following features: absolute symmetry, at least on the main fronts; an ornate entrance doorway, in the center of the facade if possible, and very often crowned with an entablature and pediment supported by pilasters or engaged columns; a bold modillioned cornice; articulation of the facade with projecting central elements, corner pilasters, or quoins; a visible roof, with dormers crowned with pediments; and occasionally a balustrade, either directly over the exterior walls or around a central roof deck. Inside such a house, there would be a spacious stair hall, often running from the front door to the back, either with two major rooms on one side or with four rooms, two on each side; the upstairs plan would be similar. All woodwork, which included carved and paneled fireplaces, would be bold and often ornate, and there might also be ornamented plasterwork in the form of cornices and centerpieces for the ceilings.

ORIGINS OF THE CLASSIC REVIVAL: ARCHAEOLOGY AND ROMANTICISM

It is perhaps not surprising that, at the end of the War of Independence in the early 1780's, some persons were receptive to the idea of an architectural style not of British origin. This was, in any case, a time of new ideas, and in Europe the doctrinaire classicism of Vitruvius, Vignola, Palladio, and Inigo Jones, based on the forms of public architecture in ancient Rome, seemed too confining, while the more venturesome forms of the Baroque period had also lost their popularity. Inspiration for new forms in architecture, decoration, and furnishings came from a number of archaeological sources. In 1754, the decorative art of Pompeii and Herculaneum was published in the *Observations sur les Antiquités de la Ville Herculaneum* of Nicolas Cochin. In 1757 the English historian Robert Wood published a monograph on the Roman ruins at Baalbek. In 1774, Charles Louis Clérisseau published *Antiquities of France*, the first serious study of Roman remains in Provence. But most important of all was *The Antiquities of Athens*, published in 1762, the fruit of four years of measuring and drawing by James Stuart and Nicholas Revett. This was the first publication to show ancient Greek architecture accurately, and its influence, both here and in Europe, was immense.

The spirit of Neoclassicism, as the style that emerged from this interest in the forms—and, in that period of rising republics, the ideals—of antiquity was called, appeared in painting and sculpture as well: the French painter David, a leading Neoclassicist, painted scenes from antiquity in ancient Roman settings, austere and recalling the work of the contemporary architects Ledoux and Boullée, with Roman costumes and furnishings correctly depicted. Ancient Greece and republican Rome were seen in an idealistic way; the aesthetic perfection of their art seemed to find a parallel in the perfection of their morality and government.

THE FEDERAL STYLE (1780–1820) IN AMERICAN ARCHITECTURE

Between 1784 and 1789, Thomas Jefferson was our minister to France. His inquiring mind turned to the Roman remains that he saw in his travels through southern France, and he was particularly attracted to the Maison Carrée, so called, a Roman Corinthian temple of 16 B.C. in Nîmes. He declared that he "gazed for hours like a lover at his mistress" at this, the best preserved of all the Roman temples. Respected for his knowledge in architectural matters, he prevailed upon the Virginia legislature to accept, as the design for their new capitol, an adaptation of the Maison Carrée worked out by Clérisseau and himself. In the capitol design, the fiction of a colonnade surrounding the building but walled in so as to leave only the porch free was retained from the temple, but the simpler Ionic order was

used and was represented in the enclosed areas by pilasters instead of half columns.

Jefferson was a self-confessed enthusiast in the arts, and he hoped, through the creation of an exemplary classical architecture, not only to educate the taste of his countrymen but also to win respect for American culture elsewhere in the world. "How is a taste for this beautiful art to be formed," he wrote Madison in 1785, "unless we avail ourselves of every occasion when public buildings are erected, of presenting to them [the public] models for their study and imitation?" Jefferson's admiration for classical architecture seems initially to have been entirely an aesthetic pleasure in its purity, stateliness, and simplicity; later, he came to admire it for ideological reasons as well, as an expression of the virtuous republics of antiquity. He was thus among the earliest exponents of the Classic Revival in America.

The finest of his executed works are his own home, "Monticello," built and rebuilt between 1769 and 1809, and the original campus of the Univer-

1. Rider House (1823), Rensselaerville, New York

This blind-arcade motif can also be found in a few surviving examples in the Western Reserve. See, for example, "Brownwood" at Bloomfield (p. 000).

THE HISTORIC BACKGROUND   211

sity of Virginia, finished in 1826. "Monticello," an elegant Palladian villa on a hilltop, has, despite new features such as the dome and the roof balustrade, some traces still of Georgian design. The university campus, long regarded as one of the supreme achievements of American architecture, is more radical and shows Jefferson's ambitions as an educator of public taste. At the head of the great elongated quadrangle he placed a domed library, closely modeled after the Pantheon at Rome. To either side are colonnades, giving access to student dormitories and to pavilions. The pavilions were designed in various orders to be "models of correct taste and architecture," and housed the professors' apartments and classrooms.

The greatest building initiated in the Federal period, although it shows traces of all periods up to and including the mid-Victorian, is the Capitol at Washington. This remarkable building has had a strange history and occupied the talents of some of the most distinguished architects available during the various phases of its construction. The site was selected by Pierre Charles L'Enfant, the artillery officer who laid out the city of Washington. A competition was held in 1792 to determine the design of the building itself. At first it appeared that a French-trained architect, Etienne Hallet, had won, but the closing date was deferred, and the ultimate winner was a physician from the West Indies, William Thornton. Hallet did indeed become Capitol architect for a while, however, acting as Thornton's successor, but was in turn succeeded by George Hadfield, who in his turn, in 1798, was succeeded by James Hoban, the architect of the White House. This succession of mainly obscure names was terminated, for a while at least, by Jefferson's appointment of one of the most distinguished figures in American architectural history, Benjamin Latrobe (1764–1820), who was Capitol architect from 1803 to 1811, and again from 1815 to 1817, when he was succeeded by another great American architect, Charles Bulfinch (1763–1844). Later, Thomas Ustick Walter was to complete the building.

The public buildings of Jefferson and the Capitol were conspicuous works in a grand style. The ordinary American built more modestly, modeling his house to some extent after the late Georgian townhouse that was appearing in London, and decorated it with ornamental work often modeled after that of the Scottish-born London architects Robert and James Adam. The Federal-style house, inside and out, had a more delicate and reserved manner, usually, than the mid-Georgian house. It might have any or all of the following features: symmetry, as in the previous period, with a central doorway if possible; a doorway with sidelights, and a semi-elliptical or semicircular fanlight covering all three sections; a light balustrade at the eaves, hiding the roof; a delicate porch, rectangular or semicircular in plan (which, after 1810, might be two-storied); bay windows, bowed or polygonal; delicate Adamesque interior ornament, with no overmantels and little if any paneling; circular or elliptical rooms; spiral staircases. The principal practitioners in New England were Charles Bulfinch of Boston, who along with his work on the Washington Capitol built state houses for Massachusetts, Connecticut, and Maine; Samuel McIntyre (1757–1811) of Salem, an architect and woodcarver famous for his quiet Adamesque ornament; Alexander Parris (1780–1852), best remembered for the simple granite Quincy Market of 1825 in Boston; and Asher Benjamin (1773–1845) who, though work of his still exists in Boston and possibly elsewhere, is best remembered for his builder's guides, which influenced the development of the Federal and the Greek Revival styles.

THE FEDERAL STYLE IN THE WESTERN RESERVE
By the time settlement in the Western Reserve became heavy—after 1815, that is—and the citizens had the leisure and prosperity to think about architecture, some foreshadowing of Greek Revival forms was often present in what they built. Many of these early houses, for instance, still have the great elliptical fanlight over the entrance door and sidelights, but in the work of Jonathan Goldsmith, the builder of Painesville, richly carved Federal ornamentation—swags, rosettes, and so on—and delicate Federal

2. Congregational Church (1829), Litchfield, Connecticut
This New England church is similar in many respects to the First Congregational Church in Tallmadge (p. 156).

3

3. First Church (1794, 1844), Windsor, Connecticut

This, an eighteenth-century church modernized on the entrance front, has a doorway of very peculiar form, but the treatment of the front as a shallow temple porch is found in the Reserve, in the First Congregational Church at Twinsburg (p. 152), for example, while the two-storied, heavily-framed tower is very similar to that of the Congregational Church at Claridon (p. 64).

half-columns are likely to decorate an essentially Greek Revival doorway with a low rectangular overdoor light. Other features characteristic of the Federal, however, remained for some years: oval pediment windows; delicate cornices resting on shallow frieze boards; now and then, tall blind arcading in shallow relief decorating part or all of a facade; and inside, attenuated pilasters, much fluting and reeding, and use of carved rosettes. The Reserve was mainly a region of timber building, naturally, in the earliest days, but there are also early brick houses, conforming more or less to town house practice in the East. The essential house was a plain structure, with none of the elliptical rooms or spiral staircases that the prosperous Easterner could afford.

The most important building in the New England village or small town was the church, and it was the church, too, that tended to dominate the Western Reserve town common. The architectural forms, however, differed: only Simeon Porter's Congregational church at Tallmadge (p. 156), of all the churches in the Reserve, resembles the elaborate Georgian and Federal churches of New England, such as that at Litchfield. Similarity with later New England work, however, is evident in the many Greek Revival churches of the Reserve.

The passage through New York state, where many eventual settlers in

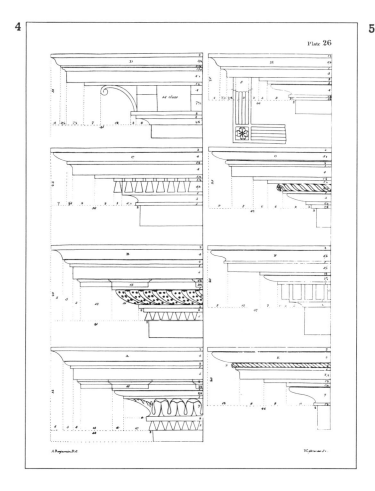

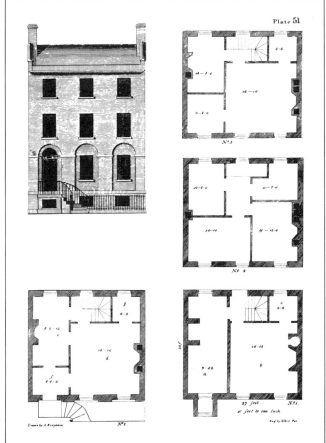

the Reserve stayed for a while, had some influence on Reserve architecture in the Federal period: the motif of the blind arcade is the most conspicuous example of such influence.

Typical of the manuals that the Western Reserve builder used for guidance is Asher Benjamin's *The American Builder's Companion*. In the 1820 edition we find the following: a section on "practical geometry"—how to taper the shaft of a column, how to set out the flutes and fillets on a pilaster, how to draw the Ionic volute; a section on the five orders of classical architecture, showing all the parts in their correct proportions; a section on cornices; a section on friezes, balusters, urns, ceiling centerpieces, and mantelpieces; and finally, plans and elevations for a town house, a church, and a courthouse. The ornamental vocabulary is still Federal, but in the fifth edition (1826) Greek forms begin to appear, and in his next book, *The Practical House Carpenter* of 1830, he publishes original and mature Grecian designs.

JONATHAN GOLDSMITH (1784–1847)

The finest builder-architect of the early Western Reserve was Jonathan Goldsmith, most of whose work was Federal but who, at the end of his career, produced some elegant Greek Revival buildings. He was born either in Milford or New Milford, Connecticut. His father, a ship captain, died at sea in 1793, leaving his mother to raise three children. At the age of eleven, Goldsmith was apprenticed to a shoemaker. At the age of seventeen he bought his freedom and apprenticed himself to a carpenter and joiner, and at twenty-one started his own building practice at Hinsdale, Massachusetts. In 1808 he married Abigail Jones, and it was from her that, at the age of twenty-four, he learned to read and write.

For information relating to Jonathan Goldsmith and his work the author is indebted to Mrs. Peter Hitchcock of Mentor, Ohio.

4. Federal-Style Cornices
These cornices, from Plate 26 of *The American Builder's Companion* (1827) by Asher Benjamin, show the thin, delicate, and yet often ornate character of detailing in the Federal period.

5. "A Small Town House"
This small brick house, illustrated in *The American Builder's Companion* (1820) by Asher Benjamin, is an example of the severe but sophisticated urban dwelling of the east coast. Certain of its characteristics may be found in the Reserve: the reliance on proportion for effect, the heavy brick parapets (in the Reserve, usually horizontal) that mask the gable ends. Even the blind arcading is present in the Reserve in at least two brick examples.

6

In 1811 Goldsmith decided to try his luck in the West. Some of Abigail's relatives had settled in Painesville, then called Champion, in the Western Reserve, and it was to this, still a frontier town, that Goldsmith moved his family. Painesville, at that time, was more populous than Cleveland and had as much promise of development. The harbor town of Fairport was close by, and the important Old State and Lakeshore roads met in Painesville itself. The Goldsmiths first occupied a log cabin, and Jonathan turned to farming and shoemaking for a livelihood. By 1818 there were six children in the family; eventually, there were to be ten.

Goldsmith's building career in the Reserve lasted from 1816 until 1838, and during that time he built not only houses but such less common structures as a bank and a lighthouse. During that time he gained a reputation for fine detailing and excellent workmanship, and the eminent citizens of Painesville and nearby towns became his clients. Some of the earliest houses on Euclid Avenue, in Cleveland, were by him.

Like other builders, Goldsmith used handbooks as a general source of inspiration. As a result, he worked in a Federal style for some time after the Greek Revival was established in the East. His Mathews, Robinson-Elwell, and Warner houses of around 1830 still have a rich Federal decoration of swags and rosettes over their doorways, supported by heavy, buttress-like volutes resting on the columns of the door frames. The Uri Seeley house of 1830, which may be by Goldsmith, has a strange overdoor pattern of radiating muntins, recalling a fanlight, over a transom with a complex curved plan. Again, the doorway of the Morley house, built as late as 1836, is still Federal in style. The low pediments of the Mathews and Robinson-Elwell houses, and the framing of the doorways in many houses so as to give sidelights and a three-part, rectangular overdoor light

6. Elevation for the Bank of Geauga (1835), Painesville

One of Jonathan Goldsmith's most important executed works and an example of his later work in the Greek Revival style, this bank was unfortunately destroyed by a fire in 1925. As executed, the corners were built out to form antae and the delicately ornamented parapet was omitted.

anticipate Greek Revival practice, however. Again, a favorite house plan of Goldsmith is one characteristic of the Greek Revival: a two-storied central block, with the entrance at the gable end, flanked by one-storied, recessed, matching wings. The Mathews house at Painesville is an example of this. Other detailing common in Goldsmith's work is the fluted trim around door and window frames, with corner blocks carved in acanthus, oak-leaf, or dogwood patterns.

By 1835, when Goldsmith began the Bank of Geauga, he was using true Greek Revival forms. The bank had paired Grecian Doric columns in antis in the entrances on its two street fronts. Drawings for a house and for a business block show him as a mature Greek Revivalist, relying on proportion and careful detailing and eschewing the ornamental elaboration of his earlier work. In 1843 he built an elegant cottage for himself, with frieze windows lighting a low attic. The grilles filling these wondows, delicately exuberant in contrast to the severity of the design of the building as a whole, were adapted from an overdoor light design that had appeared in Minard Lafever's *Modern Builder's Guide* of 1833. Unfortunately, this handsome little building burned down in the 1920's.

In 1830 Goldsmith's apprentice, Charles W. Heard, later to become a prominent architect-builder himself, married Caroline, Goldsmith's eldest daughter. The Heard-Minch house at Mentor is believed by some to have been built by Goldsmith as a wedding present. In 1836 Goldsmith lost heavily in a venture that involved laying track for the Painesville and Fairport Railroad, and the Panic of 1837 caused him further losses. In the latter year he went alone to visit his son Gillet in New Orleans, then went to Texas, where Sam Houston offered him 6,000 acres of land if he would resettle. Eventually, however, he returned to the Reserve and tried, unsuccessfully, to become the keeper of the Fairport lighthouse, the one he had built. He died in 1847.

IMPORTANT BUILDINGS BY JONATHAN GOLDSMITH

This list includes all buildings existing in 1968. Buildings no longer in existence are indicated by an asterisk.

Dr. Evert Denton House (1816)
55 Mentor Avenue, Painesville

Robert Moody House (c. 1816)
172 East South Street, Painesville
May be Goldsmith's first house in the Western Reserve.
Attribution not certain.

* "The Old Homestead" (1819), Painesville
First house built by Goldsmith for his family. Large frame house with matching one-story wings. Burned in the 1870's.

Joseph Sawyer House (c. 1820)
9364 Forsythe Road, Mentor (originally at Mentor Avenue and Chillicothe Road)
A handsome, typically Goldsmith front; fine woodwork in parlor.

Eber D. Howe House (1822)
215 Mentor Avenue, Painesville
Has been extensively altered.

*Dr. Charles P. Livingston House (c. 1826), Painesville
Greatly remodeled in the Victorian period. Demolished since 1968.

*Isaac Gillet House (c. 1827), Painesville
A red brick town house, this was one of Goldsmith's finest. It was demolished in 1958, but the doorway is on display at the Cleveland Museum of Art, and much of the woodwork is stored there.

*Judge Aaron Wilcox House (1826–28), Painesville
A brick town house in the Federal style.

Judge Reuben Hitchcock House (c. 1828)
Central block: 96 Nebraska Street, Painesville; right wing:
254 South State Street, Painesville
House has been divided.

Dr. John H. Mathews House
309 West Washington Street, Painesville
The finest existing example of a Goldsmith house.

*Col. Lemuel G. Storrs House (1825–30), Painesville
A red brick mansion with a rectangular cupola and
balustrade. Demolished in 1965. A mantel is on display at
"Lawnfield," the Garfield house in Mentor.

*Charles W. Heard (Heard-Minch) House (1830), Mentor
Although different from other Goldsmith houses, its
attribution to him seems to be accepted locally. Demolished
in 1970.

Uri Seeley House (c. 1830)
969 Riverside Drive, Painesville
Not positively attributed to Goldsmith, but the construction
in the attic resembles that of the Denton and Robinson-
Elwell houses. Good interior woodwork.

Nathan Corning House (c. 1830)
8353 Mentor Avenue, Mentor
A house on the T plan, with altered wings.

*Judge Stephen Mathews House (1831), Painesville
As fine as the John Mathews house, but disfigured at the end
by remodeling. Demolished in the 1940's.

Rider (now Lutz's) Tavern (enlargement) (1832)
792 Mentor Avenue, Painesville
The second story, a six-columned veranda, and possibly the
ells are Goldsmith's work.

*Peter M. Weddell House (c. 1832), Cleveland
A stone country house on Euclid Avenue, in the style of an
Italian villa.

Robinson-Elwell House (before 1833)
3742 Erie Street, Willoughby
One of the best examples of Goldsmith's work.

Lewis Morley House (1836)
231 North State Street, Painesville
This, the only surviving brick house by Goldsmith, is
similar in some ways to the vanished Gillet house. Originally
there was a porch across the front and a balustrade over the
eaves.

*Bank of Geauga (1835–37), Painesville
The drawings for this ambitious commercial building are in
the Western Reserve Historical Society at Cleveland. The
building itself was destroyed by fire in the 1920's.

* "Ingleside" (second Goldsmith house) (1843), Painesville
Burned in the 1920's.

7

THE GREEK REVIVAL (1820–1850) AS A NATIONAL STYLE

The earliest American building to have Grecian detailing was the Bank of Pennsylvania, built in Philadelphia in 1798 by Benjamin Latrobe. Here, Greek Ionic columns supported shallow Greek pediments over porticos at both ends of the building. Latrobe, not long in the United States, may have produced his design under the influence of the English architect Charles Robert Cockerell, with whom he had worked and who was using Grecian forms at this time.

This precocious example was not followed with any enthusiasm until 1819, when William Strickland (1787–1854), a former apprentice of Latrobe's, won the competition for the Second Bank of the United States in Philadelphia; his design included six-columned Grecian Doric porticos at either end. Strickland's busy career was nearly coterminous with the Greek Revival; later triumphs included the Merchants' Exchange of 1836, in Philadelphia, with its lantern modeled after the Choragic Monument of

7. Taylor-Lee House (1827)
New Milford, Connecticut

A house that must still be called Federal because of its detailing, but that has already the temple front usually identified with the Greek Revival.

8. Peleg Hancox House (1820)
Stonington, Connecticut

A rather small house dignified by an
Ionic portico. Such temple fronts can
be found in the Reserve—the Mitchell-
Turner house at Milan (p. 196) is a
fine example—but are nevertheless
uncommon.

Lysicrates in Athens; the Athenaeum at Providence, Rhode Island; and the
state capitol building at Nashville, Tennessee.

Other important architects of the Greek Revival period should be mentioned. Robert Mills (1781–1855) had also been in Latrobe's employ and had
assisted Jefferson in the planning of Monticello. His best-known work is
surely the Washington Monument in Washington, although this was not
executed in the elaborate manner that he had proposed, but his Washington Monument in Baltimore and his Treasury Building in Washington,
begun in 1836, are also famous. John Haviland (1792–1852) is best remembered for his Eastern State Penitentiary at Philadelphia, a design in the
Gothic style completed in 1829, but did much work in the Greek Revival
style as well and issued builder's handbooks that included Greek details.
Thomas Ustick Walter (1804–87) designed one of the most sensational
buildings of the Greek Revival, the main building of Girard College in
Philadelphia, as a huge Corinthian temple in white marble. Later, he was
to expand the Capitol in Washington, adding the Senate and House wings
and, a few years later, the dome. Minard Lafever (1798–1854) had, through
his builder's guides, a very great influence on others.

The popularity of the Greek Revival had both aesthetic and ideological
sources. The novelty and the beauty of Grecian forms would have sufficed
in themselves to capture the imagination of architects and patrons, but to
this aesthetic appeal there was added a wealth of associations with both

ancient and modern Greece. The ancient Greeks were revered for their moral and cultural perfection; the modern Greeks, fighting from 1821 until 1827 to gain their independence from the Turks, won sympathy from the new republics. Lord Byron, who first visited Greece in 1809 and who died there in 1824 while taking part in the rebellion, lent the glamor of his reputation to the new country.

The enthusiasm of the United States for the Grecian mode is represented, in an extreme form, in Nicholas Biddle of Philadelphia, who went to Greece in 1806 and was moved to write in his diary, "The two great truths in the world are the Bible and Grecian architecture." In later years he was to have a chance to demonstrate his enthusiasm: both the Second Bank of the United States and Girard College owe their temple forms to his influence, and he had Walter add a Doric portico to three sides of his own home, "Andalusia," in 1836.

New England accepted the new style less readily than did the states further south. In many villages a kind of late Georgian style survived until nearly 1850, and it was the rapidly growing shipping or manufacturing town that tended to erect banks, custom houses, mansions, and warehouses in the new style. Still, the work of Alexander Parris, Ammi B. Young, and Isiah Rogers in Boston, of Russell Warren and James Bucklin in Providence, and of Ithiel Town and Alexander Jackson Davis in New Haven are as impressive as Greek Revival work elsewhere. And the later

9. Greek Revival Porch and Doorway (1833)
The entrance of the Kirtland-Hine house in Poland (p. 117) is very nearly a literal copy of this design from *The Practice of Architecture* by Asher Benjamin, even to the quite unusual iron balustrade over the porch.

THE HISTORIC BACKGROUND   221

emigrants to the Western Reserve were not without exposure to Grecian architecture even in the villages through which they passed.

THE GREEK REVIVAL IN THE WESTERN RESERVE

The settlers who built so many of the towns of Ohio and Michigan and Illinois and Tennessee were, many of them, not the picturesque pioneers of fiction; they were solid citizens with the polished background of New England or Maryland or Virginia behind them, men who read widely and much, and whose libraries were an important part of their baggage; men brought up on the Bible and Shakespeare and Milton. They were eager readers of Byron. They were men who started academies and colleges in the town they created almost as soon as the forests had been cut down.*

The development of the Western Reserve took place just as the Greek Revival began, and the new settlers, many of them the sons and nephews of the actual purchasers of the land, quickly created cultural institutions like those they had known. Western Reserve College, one of the parent institutions of the present Case Western Reserve University, was founded in Hudson in 1826, and a few years later built the first observatory west of the Alleghenies. Oberlin College was founded in 1831. Newspapers such as the *Norwalk Reflector* and the *Ohio City Argus* were edited, as an examination of them shows, for a highly literate public. With prosperity and stability in the new territory came a demand for handsome buildings, and to meet this, craftsmen, well trained in their callings and familiar with recent stylistic developments through their builder's guides, came westward. Greek motifs published in new handbooks appeared eventually in the Western Reserve, whose architecture, if it did not equal that of the East in elaboration, was sometimes almost as advanced in taste.

The builders active in the Western Reserve during this period have left little record of themselves. Of Jonathan Goldsmith we know a considerable amount, as we do also of the Porters, Lemuel and Simeon, and of Goldsmith's son-in-law Charles Heard. Other names appear mainly in connection with individual works. The Peter Allen house and Presbyterian church in Kinsman (pp. 168–70) are attributed to Willie Smith. The Frederick Kinsman house in Warren (p. 173) is by Isaac Ladd, and Ladd may also have designed the house of Col. Simon Perkins, who was Kinsman's brother-in-law, in Akron (p. 159). Addison Kimball is remembered for the Paige house in Madison (p. 88) and for his own simple home. In Milan, the Mitchell-Turner house (p. 196) is the work of Zenas King, and the Cherry-Lockwood-Moore house (p. 198) that of Nathan Jenkins. The Sturgis-Kennan-Fulstow house in Norwalk (p. 182) is attributed by I. T. Frary

10. Detail of Greek Revival Doorway This engraving of the ornamentation for a drawing room doorway comes from *The Beauties of Modern Architecture* (1835) by Minard Lafever. It was used as inspiration by the Western Reserve builder Zenas King for the ornate entrance to the Mitchell-Turner house in Milan (p. 196).

* From Talbot Hamlin, *Greek Revival Architecture in America.*

to William Gale Meade. Despite such isolated attributions, the Greek Revival architecture of the Reserve, fine as it is, remains largely the work of anonymous builders, who translated motifs from Benjamin and Lafever to meet the means and the requirements of their clients.

Plans vary at this period, but a few standard ones appear repeatedly. The temple front, using either pilasters or freestanding columns, is frequent, as in the Allen house at Kinsman (p. 168), the Smith house near Claridon (p. 63), and the Mathews house at Painesville (p. 74). From a temple-fronted house, whose gable naturally faced the road, one or two wings, sometimes fronted with porticos, extend laterally in many cases. The Mathews house has symmetrical wings. The Ruggles-Coope house in Canfield (p. 112) is an example, rare in the Reserve, of the type of temple-fronted house most commonly associated with the Greek Revival, that in which freestanding columns form a two-story porch. A variant is the Wooster-Boalt-Overhuls house in Norwalk (p. 182), where freestanding Ionic columns in antis suggest a portico but are backed directly against the house wall. The temple front is quite rare west of the Cuyahoga River, but the Schug house at Monroeville (p. 187) has a tiny one, and the Mitchell-Turner house at Milan has a splendid one.

The earliest Greek Revival houses in the Reserve seem to have favored the use of a gable wall as a street front. In time, however, increasing numbers of houses came to be built with their axes parallel to the street. How impressive such a front could be is illustrated by the Carlisle house in Portage County (p. 132). The Selyem house at Fitchville (p. 192) shows the integration of a long porch into a house so disposed, as does the McFarlane-Reed house at Twinsburg (p. 154).

The house plan most often identified as a Western Reserve plan is that of the Barnes-Goddard house (p. 94), with a separate entry through a side wing fronted by a porch. This plan, along with certain other features—corner posts or pilasters, broad frieze boards with low windows cut into them, and large box cornices—are supposedly the constituents of a "Western Reserve Style." Actually, there is nothing particularly Western Reserve about such a combination, although many houses show some or all of these features.

Although most of the settlers in the Reserve were farmers and professional people who supplied the farmers with goods and services, the opening of canals, roads, and other means of communication caused certain towns, particularly at points of transshipment, to prosper from the sale and movement of goods. Early in its history, Cleveland was connected with the farmlands to the south by a canal, and the same was true of Milan. There were truly wealthy citizens in such communities, and houses of mansion quality were built for them. Milan and Norwalk still contain traces of the old prosperity, but the early Euclid Avenue homes by Goldsmith have long since disappeared.

The temple front, naturally, was widely used for buildings of a public character: churches, schools, courthouses, and business buildings. The Connecticut Land Company office at Warren (p. 175) and the old Mahoning County courthouse (p. 113) are examples.

Most early Western Reserve churches are explicitly Greek Revival, but some, completed as late as the 1830's, retain a Federal character. One of the most famous religious buildings in the Reserve, the Mormon temple at Kirtland (p. 84), is a case in point. Its mixture of pointed and elliptical-headed openings is merely naive, but each is, in its own way, decades behind the times. The elliptical window and door heads are Federal, as is the large oval window in the pediment, while the belfry is very nearly Colonial. Inside, the carving suggests the late 18th century. Another example is the chapel of Western Reserve Academy at Hudson (p. 144), which, though it has a temple front with Doric pilasters underneath a Greek Revival tower, has also a plain entrance where the Greek Revival would have created an elegant composition, while the side walls have two-story blind arcades, very much in the manner of certain Federal houses.

More typical, though, are churches such as those at Twinsburg (p. 152) or Weymouth (p. 121), which have temple fronts and slightly recessed belfrys, built up in two or three cubical or prismatic stages. This solemn classical architecture can be varied strangely with the introduction of Gothic openings, as in the church at Atwater (p. 126) or that at Claridon (p. 64).

ROMANTICISM

Even as the Greek Revival flourished, other styles appeared in American architecture. Just as today we see buildings erected in a variety of styles, with "modern" of various sorts predominating but with an occasional pseudo-Colonial bank or Gothic church appearing too, so Americans of the 1830's saw an occasional Gothic house or church among the commoner classical work being erected. The seeds of the Gothic Revival, this new style, were English. Already, around 1600, the Middle Ages had been seen as a subject for romantic literary treatment and pageantry, and some hundred years later Sir Christopher Wren and Nicholas Hawksmoor were to produce Gothic designs—Hawksmoor's towers for Westminster Abbey are an example—either to complete unfinished medieval buildings or to reflect the medieval associations of certain sites. In the early eighteenth century, the owners of country houses began to see in medieval ruins, authentic or false, and in small Gothic garden pavilions a way of lending interest to their estates and of providing, through what was regarded as curious, rather barbaric design, a relief from the somewhat boring certainties of the prevailing Palladian style. Sir John Vanbrugh, who designed Blenheim Palace and other country houses in a grandiose Baroque manner, was also sensitive to the associative values in medieval English architecture; he pleaded for the preservation of a medieval ruin on the grounds of Blenheim, and designed a number of houses which, though not Gothic, had the rugged and complex aspect of a castle.

The first true Gothic Revival house is usually assumed to be "Strawberry Hill," the country villa of Horace Walpole near London. Decorated inside with motifs adapted from an incongruous variety of medieval examples, "Strawberry Hill" was playful in treatment and intention. William

Beckford's mansion, "Fonthill Abbey," designed some 45 years later and erected on the edge of the Salisbury Plain, shows a highly theatrical striving after a more serious effect. It was built to suggest a convent, partly in ruins but still partly habitable. These two buildings suggest the range of attitude that the eighteenth century had toward the Gothic. It had novelty, and a slightly perverse charm, through its disregard of classical principles. It had about it the thrill of association with remote British history. And it could be used to create a mood, particularly one of melancholy or horror—and both Walpole and Beckford were the authors of "Gothic" romances. It was for the nineteenth century to institutionalize Gothic, to make of it as it did a symbol of national culture, of the Christian religion, or of all that was sound and honest in architecture. When the competition for the new Houses of Parliament which were to replace those burned in 1834 was held, the rules stated that the new buildings must be in Elizabethan or Gothic, that is, in styles of a "national" character. The executed work owed its general composition to Charles Barry, a classicist, and its detailing to Augustus N. W. Pugin, a passionate and sensitive Gothicist; together they produced a work in which their varied talents were employed to good effect. Around the same time, a concern with the state of religion in England led to the building of Gothic churches which, gaining rapidly in stylistic correctness, came, for some elements in the Church of England at least, to seem an indispensable setting for Christian worship. Again, John Ruskin and a number of Victorian architects found in Gothic architecture of one kind or another the peculiar combination of richness, constructive soundness, and truthful expression of construction that their theories demanded.

THE GOTHIC REVIVAL IN THE UNITED STATES

In the United States this triple impetus was considerably weaker. Nationalism was not involved. The feeling that Gothic was the natural style for religion was there, certainly, and the presence of Gothic windows in many an essentially Federal or Greek Revival church—a peculiarity not confined to the Western Reserve—is evidence of the vitality of the Gothic window as a symbol. Again, some architects turned to medieval forms as sound, rational, and honest. But for the most part it was the pictorial quality of Gothic, its ability to fit harmoniously into a setting of mountains, hills, or woods, that attracted architects. Andrew Jackson Downing (1815–52), a widely influential landscape architect and writer on horticulture, popularized the Gothic house designs of Alexander Jackson Davis (1803–92), and Calvert Vaux (1824–95) who, with many other architects, produced Gothic houses from the 1830's on that ranged from simple cottages, clad with vertical board-and-batten siding and announcing their stylistic affiliation only with simple vergeboards and a pointed window or two, up to mock castles of stone, towered and gloomy, with stained glass and richly carved furniture.

Perhaps the first Gothic Revival work in the United States was "Sedgeley," a house of around 1800 by Latrobe. In 1805 he prepared an alternative Gothic design for a Baltimore cathedral, and in 1808 built a Gothic bank in Philadelphia. The first Gothic religious building actually executed in the United States was the chapel of St. Mary's Seminary in Baltimore (1807) by Maximilian Godefroy, and the first Gothic Revival cathedral was begun two years later by Joseph Mangin in New York. Haviland's Eastern State Penitentiary has already been mentioned. Such early work was not yet "true" Gothic; the "authentic" Gothic style appeared only later, with Davis' villa and church designs and with the church architecture of Richard Upjohn (1802–78) and James Renwick (1818–95). Perhaps its masterpiece is Renwick's St. Patrick's Cathedral in New York, begun in 1857. Minard Lafever, usually associated with Greek Revival work of the greatest elegance and clarity, worked in other styles at the end of his career, and in the Church of the Holy Trinity, begun in Brooklyn in 1844, produced a major Gothic Revival work of somber richness.

ECLECTICISM BEFORE THE CIVIL WAR

Other styles were introduced, again from England, after 1830. The Norman Romanesque style was, once again, a "national" style which, in its imported form, was popular for churches and villas. The Smithsonian Institution in Washington, begun in 1846 by James Renwick, is a distinguished example of this style. A mild Egyptian revival took place as well, and produced a few churches, although its main application was to places where an effect of mass and gloom seemed important: cemetery entrances, prisons—John Haviland's Tombs prison in New York, begun in 1836, is an outstanding example—and, in at least one instance, a reservoir wall. The "Moorish" style appeared now and again, and was used for at least one great villa, that of P. T. Barnum in Bridgeport, Connecticut.

The major rival to the Greek Revival from about 1840 on, and its eventual successor, was the "Tuscan" or "Italian Villa" style. By replacing the gable roof of the Greek Revival with a shallow hipped or flat roof, carried well beyond the walls on fancifully shaped brackets, the Tuscan style created a volume of fully utilizable space. Again, it was possible, in the Tuscan style, to raise absolutely unadorned walls, relying on the entrance, the cornice, and perhaps arched window heads for decoration. Furthermore, it permitted a picturesque grouping of elements, creating a plan whose irregular perimeter would have been unthinkable in the Greek Revival. There were numerous practical reasons, therefore, for its increasing popularity.

A refinement of the plain, cubical Tuscan villa was the octagon house. In the 1840's Orson Fowler, a phrenologist by profession, wrote a little book, *A Home for All,* in which he demonstrated arithmetically that the most economical and convenient house to build is some viable approximation of a sphere. He settled upon a house with an octagonal plan, two or three stories high, and created a vogue that lasted through the 1850's.

Finally, there was a Renaissance revival, most in evidence in business buildings and other urban structures where an effect of opulence was desired. One interesting building type that usually appeared in a Renaissance form was the store building with the cast-iron front. James Bogardus, a New York inventor, erected the first of these self-supporting fronts, assembled from iron castings, in 1848, and they quickly came into use everywhere in the country where multi-storied commercial buildings were needed. Their vogue lasted about 25 years.

An architect of the 1840's or later was likely to practice in more than one of these styles. Lafever, besides Grecian and Gothic work, produced Egyptian and Italianate designs. Richard Upjohn designed Italian villas and Romanesque churches as well as Gothic ones. Samuel Sloan (1815–84), a truly eclectic architect, published designs in the Gothic, Greek, Tuscan, Norman, and Moorish styles, as well as some in styles that were more or less original inventions. Alexander Jackson Davis worked in Greek, Gothic, and various Italian manners. The 1840's and 1850's were a restless, venturesome period, whose products are not to everyone's taste.

GOTHICISM AND ECLECTICISM IN THE WESTERN RESERVE

The new styles came to the Reserve somewhat belatedly, and in their application to local means and requirements they were stripped of many of their Romantic elaborations. The books of Downing, Vaux, and Sloan were doubtless consulted, but their ideas were in the main simplified. The church at Kirtland (p. 83) is unusual in its elaborate and rather heavy use of ornamental motives that seem to be derived from Sloan.

An early example of the Gothic Revival in the Western Reserve is St. John's Historic Episcopal Church in Cleveland (p. 37), finished in 1837. Built in Ohio City, now a part of Cleveland's West Side, it remains a charming, primitive piece of history, even though it has now lost its finials. Another early survivor is the First Congregational Church of Elyria, built in 1848, with its squat crenelated towers of rubble. In 1848, again, St. Paul's Church in Cleveland, designed by the local firm of Heard and Porter, was erected. No longer in existence, it is of interest because it appears to have been modeled after Upjohn's Trinity Church, built only two years before. Heard and Porter also produced a handsome Romanesque church which survives on Public Square in Cleveland, the First Presbyterian ("Old Stone") Church (p. 30).

The domestic Gothic Revival has left few traces. Among the best of the surviving examples are the Wing-McAdoo-Kennedy house in Bloomfield (p. 172), which shows the influence of Downing, and the C. R. Howard house at Aurora (p. 127), less purely Gothic but interesting for its cobblestone facing. More humble, though handsome in its own way, is the board-and-batten house from Ashtabula County shown on page 24.

The Tuscan style is much more common; it had a wide use in the Reserve until 1870. The Cahoon-Amidon house in Lorain County (p. 105) is an early and good example of the style, showing its typical features. The Roft house in Sandusky (p. 200) shows the cupola that is often found, while the Lockwood house at Milan (p. 199) is an example of a Tuscan villa that was later modernized by the addition of a mansard roof and a tower. Cleveland still has a number of Tuscan houses, the Merwin house (p. 39) being one of the best.

The use of cast iron in commercial architecture is limited, although one or two cast-iron fronts survive in Cleveland. More common is the open store front supported on iron columns that is found in the Kelley Block at Milan (p. 194) or Hoyt's Department Store at North Fairfield (p. 190).

HEZEKIAH ELDREDGE (1795–1845)

To the best of our knowledge, only one building by Hezekiah Eldredge is still standing: St. John's Historical Episcopal Church, located on the "near West Side" of Cleveland. Although so little remains of his work, Eldredge's life is interesting as typifying the careers of the early builders in the Western Reserve.

Until 1825 Eldredge was a citizen of Weedsport, New York, working as a carpenter and joiner. In that year he moved to Rochester, a town, at that time, of nine thousand persons, and there constructed a number of important buildings. He had a son who had settled in Brooklyn, Ohio, an area later to be called Ohio City and still later to become the "near West Side" of Cleveland. This son persuaded Eldredge to move to Brooklyn. On his arrival in 1834 he was given the commission to rebuild a manufacturing plant beside the Cuyahoga River. Other commissions followed quickly. This was a period of intense land speculation, and the demand for buildings was heavy. For the Buffalo Company, which controlled a large tract of land, Eldredge built the Ohio City Exchange, a complex that included stores, offices, and a hotel. An elaborate building, it contained, besides the usual rooms of a hotel at that period, a ballroom that was a social center of Ohio City until the demolition of the hotel in 1850. The bedrooms were richly paneled in cherry and mahogany, and much of the wood for the building was shipped from the East. For James S. Clark, proprietor of the "Willeyville" tract, Eldredge built a commercial block, the Cleveland Center Block, to attract business. For Josiah Barber and Richard Lord, who held much of the land between the Buffalo Company and Willeyville tracts, he built another hotel, the Pearl Street House, at a cost of some nine thousand dollars; this hotel was destroyed by fire in 1855.

St. John's, built in 1837, is today in much its original exterior form, the main alteration being the loss of its finials. The interior, however, has had to be rebuilt twice, once after a fire in 1866 and once after a tornado in 1953. Of the church the *Ohio City Argus* wrote, shortly before its opening:

It is a source of pleasure to ourselves as well as to the citizens of this place generally to see so fine a structure as St. John's certainly is, be created. We have

---

For information on the life of Eldredge I am indebted to the manuscript by Sarah Rusk (No. 3259) at the Western Reserve Historical Society, Cleveland.

11   12

looked with much interest towards its completion as an edifice that would do honor to this or any other city, and thus far we have not been disappointed.... It is another example of the characteristic enterprise of our people and shows that notwithstanding the efforts of some to retard the growth of this place, Ohio City is advancing in its course of prosperity with a rapidity surpassed by few places in the United States.

The building has been erected by the Episcopal Society of this City and is expected to be ready for occupancy by next Christmas. It is built of unhewn rubble stone with one gallery for the choir. It is designed to accommodate about 600 persons, and the estimated expense of the building is about $11,000. Hezekiah Eldredge, the architect, favors us with the following dimensions: outside: 85′ x 50′; tower to ground: 87′; minarets above tower: 24. The minarets are furnished with windows and can be illuminated on every public occasion.

Eldredge became a leading citizen of the small community. Many carpenters and joiners learned their trades with him. Surprisingly, though, he had to file a petition of bankruptcy in 1842. He continued in business, however, and at the time of his death in 1845 he was building the Vineyard Lane Bridge over the Ohio Canal.

LEMUEL PORTER (c. 1775–1829) AND SIMEON PORTER (1807–71)

Two other important builders of the early Western Reserve were the Porters, father and son, whose work, individually and collectively, spanned the Federal, Greek Revival, and early Victorian periods.

When Lemuel Porter came from Waterbury, Connecticut to Tallmadge in 1818, he was over forty years old. He was a woodworker, and in 1821

11., 12. A Western Reserve Gable and Its Precedent

While we cannot be sure, this vergeboard and the lancet-traceried window framed by it seem to be a simplified version of this gable design from Plate 104 of *The Model Architect* (1860) by Samuel Sloan.

228   *THE HISTORIC BACKGROUND*

13   14

was engaged to build the First Congregational Church at Tallmadge (p. 156). This church, with its mixture of Georgian and Federal elements, is virtually unique in the Western Reserve.

In 1825 Lemuel Porter was appointed to a committee to find a site for Western Reserve College, then being organized, and the next year received a contract to erect its first building on the new site at Hudson. This "Middle College," a plain brick block with parapet gables and a domed cylindrical belfry, has long been demolished. In March of 1829 he was given the contract for another college building long since gone, and for the building now known as the President's House (p. 145). Later in the year, however, Lemuel Porter died, and Simeon was engaged to complete the buildings. In 1834 he was awarded the contract for the college chapel (p. 144), which survives in a somewhat altered form, and by 1843 had built three other buildings for the college, which still exist: North College, the Observatory (p. 149), and the Athenaeum (p. 147). During this time Porter was building outside the college too, both in the town of Hudson and elsewhere. "The Elms," the Brewster house (p. 150), is certainly his work, and the Nutting house (p. 146) is certainly good enough to be his. Two of his churches, a Greek Revival one in Brecksville and a Gothic one in Hudson, have been lost to fire, but it is possible that he was the designer of the church at Streetsboro, now at the Hale Homestead.

In 1848 Porter moved to Cleveland, and shortly thereafter joined Charles Wallace Heard, the son-in-law of Jonathan Goldsmith, in an architectural partnership. In the first three years, Heard and Porter designed three important churches, of which only one, the Romanesque "Old Stone" church

13., 14. Romanesque Detailing of the 1850's

The Old South Church at Kirtland (p. 83) may be a simplified wooden version of this masonry church from Plate 77 of *The Model Architect*. Plate 41 from the same book, showing detailing for a mansion in the Norman style, may have supplied ideas for the doorway of Old South Church and the heavy ornamental banding above it.

(p. 30), survives. This, however, is likely to have been Heard's design, as Porter, up to this time, had almost consistently worked in some sort of classical idiom. Other works of the partnership were the Hinman B. Hurlburt house of 1855 on Euclid Avenue, a Tuscan mansion with a precociously High Victorian diaper pattern in its brickwork; the old Central High School of 1856, a large Romanesque building with cast-iron columns as part of its interior structure; and the principal building for Lake Erie Female Seminary, now the Lake Erie College for Women (p. 76) in 1859, probably the largest building the partnership designed.

Heard and Porter was dissolved in 1860, and Porter set up a practice of his own. In 1861 he was at work on another Cleveland high school, and that year also received the contract for College Hall, now Chapman Hall, at Mount Union College in Alliance. The Congregational church in Hudson, (p. 149), a Gothic building completed in 1865, was also his work. His last recorded work was Miller Hall at Mount Union College. He died in 1871 at the age of 64. Happily, much of his work remains to be seen in the Western Reserve.

AMERICAN ARCHITECTURE AFTER THE CIVIL WAR

The decades that followed the Civil War saw the eclecticism that had preceded it continue, develop further, and end in a kind of wayward originality. This was a time of new wealth, and the possessor of such wealth, often a man without much culture or education, was likely to demand architecture that impressed through size and complexity rather than architecture that had stylistic correctness.

Lewis Mumford, in *The Brown Decades,* was moved to write:

Looking back over the previous hundred years to the time when there was but one professional architect in the whole country, one might have made the generalization that, as the number of architects increased, the number of satisfactory buildings had proportionately diminished.

Not all of the post-Civil War architects deserved such censure, however. While most American architects of this period had been trained in the offices and drawing schools, in the old manner, a few of the new architects had studied in schools abroad—in 1865 we had no architectural schools of our own. By far the most influential of the foreign schools was the École des Beaux-Arts in Paris, from which some of our most distinguished architects have graduated. Already before the Civil War, Richard Morris Hunt, later to be known for his mansions in New York and Newport, had returned from the Beaux-Arts to practice in New York. And directly after the war, one of our very greatest architects, Henry Hobson Richardson (1838–86) returned from the school to set up an office, first in New York, later in Brookline, Massachusetts. For several years Richardson worked hesitantly in a number of styles, still finding himself as an artist, but his Brattle Square Church of 1872 in Boston was already a firmly composed work in the Romanesque manner with which his name is associated, and Trinity Church, Boston, finished in 1877, made him one of the most famous and influential architects ever to have practiced in this country. In his busy career, which terminated with his premature death at age 48, his office planned houses, public buildings, churches, and commercial buildings which, for some years after his death, were imitated, for better or worse, everywhere in the country. He is best known for buildings like the Allegheny County courthouse and jail (1884–88) at Pittsburgh—heavy, round-arched buildings of rock-faced masonry—but he was an early, and great, creator of houses in the Shingle Style—low-lying, shingle-clad houses beneath great spreading roofs.

Richardson's Marshall Field wholesale store (1885–87; now destroyed) in Chicago was a particularly interesting example of his commercial work, since it showed his approach to the vexed problem of the many-storied building. Ordinarily, a Victorian architect, confronted with vast wall areas of such a great boxlike structure as the Field store, attempted arbitrary vertical and horizontal subdivisions which he would then treat individually; he thus created, almost inevitably, an irrational and disunified facade. Richardson, although his treatment of the problem here did not result in a completely consistent architectural system, emphasized the essential boxiness of the building and divided the greater part of the solid masonry wall into a structural arcade with recessed, screen-like areas. The more rationalistic skyscrapers to come would maintain this division of structure and screen, translating the masonry forms into those of fireproofed steelwork, making the elevation a unified expression of the structural system, and of course heightening the building immensely.

Richardson never lived to build a skeleton-framed commercial building. It was left for John Wellborn Root (1850–91) and Daniel H. Burnham (1846–1912), and particularly for Louis Sullivan (1856–1924) to evolve logical treatments of this new building type, emphasizing in some cases the grid-like character of the frame and in others the verticality, the tower-like quality, of the mass.

The eclecticism of the post-Civil War period, in the meantime, began in the 1870's to acquire a polish and correctness equal or superior to that of the best work of the 1840's. The Centennial Exhibition of 1876 made Americans aware of the architecture and decorative work being produced in Europe, and especially of the charming "Queen Anne" style then current in England, whose free mixture of motifs united in whimsical ways the seventeenth and eighteenth centuries with the medieval and the Japanese. At the same period, our Colonial architecture, as a symbol of our origins, caught the fancy of the public. The result of this exposure to styles of architecture thus far unfamiliar to many laymen and many architects alike was to create a mood of experimentation and a general feeling that the prevailing standards of design and workmanship had to be upgraded. As increasing numbers of architects were exposed to academic training, either abroad or in our own newly established schools, as increasing numbers of students traveled, as architectural magazines appeared, as photography made it possible to see the exact form and texture of a building without travel, a powerful impetus developed for the creation of a sensuous, sophisticated architecture which, with the passage of time, became, almost inevitably, more and more dependent upon specific stylistic precedents. Charles Follen McKim (1847–1909), a Beaux-Arts graduate and a former draftsman in Richardson's studio, and Stanford White (1853–1906), who had also worked for Richardson, became perhaps the most important architects of the new eclecticism. Working at first in the Richardsonian and Shingle Style manners, they soon evolved a free pseudo-Colonial residential style and a fifteenth-century Italian style which they used in city houses, commercial buildings, and churches. At the time of their deaths, in the mid-1900's, their firm of McKim, Mead and White was immensely successful, producing works of imperial Roman grandeur at a more-than-Roman scale.

WESTERN RESERVE ARCHITECTURE AFTER THE CIVIL WAR

During the 1860's Cleveland had had a remarkable growth—from somewhat over 43,000 persons in 1860 to approximately 93,000 in 1870, and this growth continued; by 1900 Cleveland was a city of 382,000. The latter half of the nineteenth century saw it not only an important lake port but also a steelmaking and manufacturing town. In the center of the city business buildings of unprecedented size arose, while the frame houses of the factory workers spread over the lowland areas of the East Side and beyond the borders of the old Ohio City. As one passed through Cleveland, these undistinguished homes, and the mills their inhabitants served, were most in evidence, but the Richardsonian Arcade (p. 34), and the Society for Savings Building (p. 32), by John Wellborn Root, were buildings in which the city might take pride as the century drew toward its close.

For the newly wealthy, Euclid Avenue on the East Side, favored even before the war, and Franklin Avenue on the West Side offered tempting house sites. The favored style for the new mansions was a kind of Second Empire French, which produced houses that were often no more than heavily ornamented versions of the pre-war Tuscan villa, with a mansard roof instead of a flat one. Gothic also appeared: a heavy and elaborate Gothic, usually, without the delicacy and economy of the pre-war examples. The most successful firm of the immediate post-war period was Heard and Blythe, whose partners were Charles Heard, now separated from Simeon Porter, and his son-in-law Walter Blythe. Their residential work in Cleveland, however, has virtually disappeared, and indeed, it is generally outside Cleveland that one must look for examples of the large mid-Victorian house.

As usual, new styles came into general use in the Reserve after a lag of a few years. The Tuscan villa type, more elaborately decorated than before but essentially the same, persisted for some time. "Jennings Place," by Heard and Blythe (p. 81), is a restrained work, essentially pre-war. The Kent-Warner house at Wellington (p. 99) has true mid-Victorian elaboration, but remains nearly cubical, flat-roofed, and cupola-crowned. The John Olmstead house at Conneaut (p. 18), built in 1878, has a tower capped with a mansard roof, but the remainder of the building is still Tuscan.

The mansard roof appeared in its full Second Empire elaboration as early as 1869, though, in the Hower-Crawford house at Akron (p. 160). Here, in fact, is an indication of how the Reserve had changed over fifty years. The pioneer simplicity of a new agricultural community, satisfied with the spare elegance of a plain wooden house with Federal detailing, is gone; here is an up-to-date, cosmopolitan house, with a sophisticated plan, elaborate woodwork, and exotic furnishings: a house that symbolizes a desire to display wealth and to be linked culturally with the world beyond the Reserve. The Hart house (p. 106) at Oberlin reflects, in a much humbler way, the desire to be in fashion.

The village of Chagrin Falls, which prospered in the 1870's and '80's from water-driven mills, retains much architecture from this period. The Tuscan villa, its rectangular perimeter varied by one or more polygonal bay windows, is common. The Stoneman-Nokes house (p. 54) is a typical example, plain despite the elaborate detailing of its porch.

At this time, power machinery, particularly the power-driven jigsaw, had increased the temptation to decorate buildings, inside and out, with elaborate woodwork. Crisp cut-out patterns, executed in jigsawn boards, whether superimposed to create three-dimensional forms or used as a two-dimensional lacework, became so cheap that anyone who built could afford a few brackets under his eaves or a fancy decorative area in the apex of his gable. The Winans house in Madison (p. 90) is an example of this kind of work. Turnings also became very popular, especially after 1880, and the Holsey Gates house at Bedford, begun in 1891, shows the extent to which turnings were used. The plain clapboard surfaces are a traditional American form of siding, but both the outline and the fenestration of this house are picturesquely varied, and the interior shows the massive richness and elaborate working that characterizes the joinery of this period.

The Shingle Style is less common and lacks the sophistication of the best work along the New England and New Jersey shores, but the Hine house at Mantua (p. 136) is one prominent example.

CHARLES F. SCHWEINFURTH (1856–1919)

In Western Reserve mansions built in the 1880's, particularly in Cleveland, H. H. Richardson's Romanesque manner was highly influential, and no architect in the Reserve used it to better effect than Charles F. Schweinfurth in his early work. He was born in Auburn, New York, in 1856. After graduating from high school in 1872 he spent two years in technical study, then entered the office of a prominent New York architect. In 1875 he became supervising architect of the U.S. Treasury Department, but, "not being in sympathy with the restraint and methods of government architecture," left in 1881 to take charge of an architect's office. This may have been the New York office of H. H. Richardson, although there is no certainty on the matter.

In 1883 he received a commission to design the Euclid Avenue mansion of Sylvester Everett, and it was this commission that brought him, at the age of twenty-seven, to a practice in Cleveland. For a short while Schweinfurth entered into a partnership with his brother Julius, but this soon ended. The Everett house (pp. 238, 246), which the brothers designed together, was the greatest built in Cleveland up to that time and one of the greatest ever built in the city. It was in a pure Richardsonian style, and Richardson himself praised it highly. Schweinfurth continued in the Romanesque manner through the 1880's, as his Chisholm house of 1887 (p. 242) shows. In 1887 too he began the Calvary Presbyterian Church (p. 41), with its massive towers and great entrance arch and its complex side elevation. The round arches, rock-faced ashlar, mountainous roofs, and towering chimneys of the Romanesque Revival style appealed to him, although to the Richardsonian features that he used he often added a massive corner tower. The interiors, of course, contained richly carved woodwork. Schweinfurth became known as a perfectionist; he built expensively, but saw to it that materials and workmanship were of the highest quality, and his clients appreciated this.

In 1894 Schweinfurth built an interesting house, square and fortress-like, for himself (p. 42). The crenelated street front shows, in an austere way, the transition that he was making at that period to the Gothic. The entrance is charming, with its bluntly pointed archway, its exquisitely wrought lantern, and its intricately worked door. In 1896 the architect turned to classicism for his Backus Law School at Western Reserve University (p. 44). He was to build other work for the University, mainly in

For further information regarding Schweinfurth, see Ph.D. thesis by Regina Perry, WG-378.771-OP 462, in the I. F. Freiberger Library, Case Western Reserve University, Cleveland.

15. McClymonds House (1893)
Massillon

One of Charles Schweinfurth's best, the John Walter McClymonds house is not actually in the Reserve, though it is close by. At this point Schweinfurth was still working more or less in the Romanesque style, but other stylistic influences, typical for the eclecticism of the period, are apparent as well: the arches are a bluntly pointed Gothic, the crenelation is Tudor, and the third-floor balcony is French Renaissance.

the Tudor manner that was to be his favorite in the latter part of his career. In 1900 he was commissioned to do a series of massive stone bridges to carry traffic over Liberty Boulevard, a road that winds through a Cleveland park. These bridges are all different, but all have a rugged quality that suits the wild setting beautifully.

Schweinfurth designed in a variety of styles, but his favorite period, in his later years, was the late English Gothic. Most of his work at Western Reserve University (pp. 44–47) was Tudor, and so was his design for one of the greatest and latest of the Euclid Avenue houses, still standing, the Samuel Mather house (p. 46). This last was perhaps the most imposing and most expensive house ever built in Cleveland; even today, stripped of its landscaping and its great entrance marquee, it is impressive. His greatest work is Trinity Cathedral, finished in 1907, an English Perpendicular work in Indiana limestone, with rich detailing outside and inside.

Schweinfurth's personality was a mixture of uncompromising perfectionism and sentiment. The former quality led to the loss of sight in one eye, during a quarrel with a plasterer whose work he had destroyed, finding it inferior. The latter trait is shown by the following story, told by Episcopal bishop Leonard in 1919:

After a long session with the Building Committee in which Mr. Schweinfurth seemed to plead in vain for the necessary funds with which to erect the tower and thus complete his masterpiece, Mr. Samuel Mather started to withdraw from the conference on the plea of having another engagement. At the door he stopped and said, "Gentlemen, it will be unnecessary for you further to study means by which the Trustees may secure the necessary funds with which to erect the tower, I have decided to erect same in memory of my father." Mr. Mather at once disappeared. After members of the Committee had ceased to congratulate one another on the happy outcome of their struggle, they looked about for Schwein-furth in order to give him the necessary instructions for proceedings with the work, but he had disappeared. After a long search, the Bishop found him in the Parish house to which he had retired in order to give way to tears of satis-faction and gratitude.

Of him a fellow-architect, Benjamin Hubbell, said:

He was known as a man of the highest integrity and when he was not embittered from lack of appreciation by clients and contractors, always exhibited the most loveable and generous disposition. He was recognized in Cleveland and through-out the country as an architect with the deepest regard for professional ethics, and was admired for his sterling integrity and for his uncompromising deter-mination to secure for his clients that to which, by reason of their contracts, they were justly entitled. There can be no question but that his personality, more than that of any other man, has tended to raise the standard of architec-tural design and construction in Cleveland and though he has passed away, his works will remain for us for many years as an example of the high ideals for which he stood.

Of himself, Schweinfurth said:

I hold my former masters in deepest respect, very often recalling their fine words and sympathy, thereby receiving renewed enthusiasm and a striving for higher ideals. I have always studied out my problems making my own designs, going over all the details and superintending my own work, knowing what I want and recognizing it when seen, so you may know that my life has been a happy and busy one, if at times architecturally lonely.

IMPORTANT BUILDINGS BY CHARLES F. SCHWEINFURTH

Many of these buildings are illustrated in this book; no additional comments are supplied for these. All addresses are in Cleveland unless otherwise noted. Demolished buildings are indicated by an asterisk.

*Sylvester T. Everett House (1883)
Euclid Avenue

Old Stone Church (remodeling, 1884)
Public Square

Garfield Memorial Competition (1884)
Schweinfurth's design was not used.

*William Chisholm House (1887)
Euclid Avenue

Calvary Presbyterian Church (1887–90)
Euclid Avenue at East 79th Street

*Lennox Apartments (1889–90)
Euclid Avenue
Demolished in the 1920's to make way for the
Union Commerce Building.

*Harry K. Devereux House (c. 1890)
Euclid Avenue

People's Savings and Loan Company (1890)
Franklin Avenue at West 25th Street
This building has been reduced to two stories; originally it
was partly four, partly six stories high.

*J. E. French House (1890)
Euclid Avenue
A Romanesque design.

"Shoreby" (1890)
Lake Shore Boulevard, Bratenahl, Ohio
A mansion in one of Cleveland's suburbs, splendidly sited
beside Lake Erie.

*John L. Severance House (1891–92)
Euclid Avenue
The Severances were one of Cleveland's eminent families.

*Ursuline Convent (1893)
East 55th Street
An impressive Romanesque construction, much admired
in its time.

*W. H. Boardman House (1893)
Euclid Avenue

John Walter McClymonds House (1893)
Massillon, Ohio

Charles F. Schweinfurth House (1894)
1951 East 75th Street

New England Building (1895)
Euclid Avenue near East 6th Street
Now occupied by National City Bank of Cleveland.
The ground floor was remodeled by the local firm of Walker
and Weeks in the 1920's.

Old Physics Building (1895)
Adelbert College, Case Western Reserve University
A massive red-brick building with interestingly detailed
blunt Gothic arches.

*Hatch Library (1895–98)
Western Reserve University
A Tudor building, demolished around 1960.

Backus Law School (1896)
Case Western Reserve University

*Cleveland Telephone Company Building (before 1897)
West 3rd Street
Demolished in the 1920's to make way for the
Terminal Tower complex.

*American Trust Building (before 1897)
Public Square
Either destroyed or altered out of recognition.

F. F. Prentiss House (c. 1897)
8811 Euclid Avenue
A large house, still partly visible in the Ingleside
Hospital complex.

*David Z. Norton House (1897–98)
Euclid Avenue

Bridges over Liberty Boulevard (1900–1)

Trinity Cathedral (1901–7; parish house 1890–95)
Euclid Avenue at East 22nd Street

Haydn Hall (1902)
Flora Stone Mather College, Case Western
Reserve University

Harkness Chapel (1902)
Flora Stone Mather College, Case Western
Reserve University

Mary Chisholm Painter Arch (1904)
Flora Stone Mather College, Case Western
Reserve University

Union Club (1906)
Euclid Avenue at East 12th Street
An Italianate design showing influence from Stanford
White's design for the Metropolitan Club in New York.

Samuel Mather House (1907–10)
2605 Euclid Avenue

Ransom Hall (1910)
Kenyon College, Gambier, Ohio
A crenelated Tudor building.

Flora Stone Mather College (main building, 1912)
Case Western Reserve University
A brick-and-stone Tudor building with rich carving.

Cuyahoga County Courthouse (second floor courtrooms
and bronze entrance doors, 1912)
Lakeside Avenue
The building architects were Lehman and Schmidt, but
certain details were turned over to Frank Haushka
of Schweinfurth's office.

University School (original building; date unknown)
Hough Avenue at East 71st Street
Too small for present-day needs, this building is now
threatened with demolition.

*C. E. Briggs House (date unknown)
Overlook Road
An impressive Tudor mansion occupying an entire city
block; demolished in the 1960's.

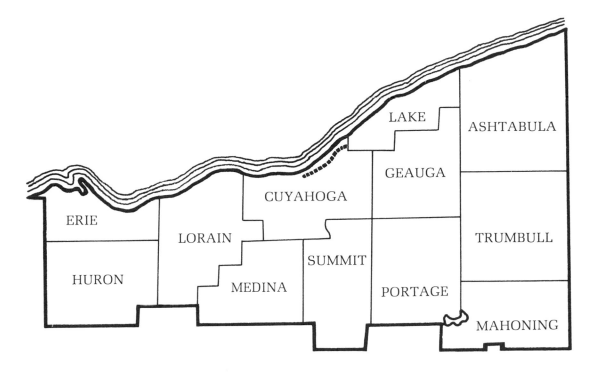

EUCLID AVENUE

A STREET OF MANSIONS IN VICTORIAN CLEVELAND

This book is primarily concerned with the architecture of the Western Reserve that still exists. It seems well, however, at least to look briefly at a phenomenon, now vanished forever, that was the Reserve's proudest architectural display: Euclid Avenue. Here the merchant princes of Cleveland had their mansions, with lawns, trees, and gardens. Toward the avenue's western end the business district and the tall buildings began, while beyond Fortieth Street the avenue had the sleepy, tree-lined look of a small-town street. The earliest of the large houses, some of them by Goldsmith, were built when the city was still a regional trading center with a population of a few thousands; the last were built for manufacturers, merchants, and bankers in a city of nearly half a million. Until after World War I the avenue retained its greatness; that the immense Samuel Mather house and Trinity Cathedral could be built there after 1900 was an indication of continuing confidence that the wealthy had in the future of the street.

By 1940, there was scarcely a trace of the old grandeur. The mansions had disappeared or deteriorated, and Euclid Avenue had become a chaotic and gloomy street. We present here a selection of photographs from the extensive collection of the Western Reserve Historical Society, Cleveland, showing Euclid Avenue as it was. Except for the Samuel Mather house, which appears in one view, all these houses have been destroyed.

Sylvester T. Everett House. The porte-cochere shows the handsome, massive masonry characteristic of Schweinfurth's work during his entire career and the Richardsonian stone carving and polychrome inlay of this period.

239

1

240   EUCLID AVENUE

1. R. K. Winslow House (c. 1878)
Euclid Avenue at 24th Street
No more outstanding example of High
Victorian architecture existed in
Cleveland than this mansion, on the
present site of Cleveland State
University.

2. Harry K. Devereux House (c. 1890)
Euclid Avenue east of 26th Street
Here, Schweinfurth's Richardsonian
manner is apparent in the rock-faced
ashlar, the massive roofs, and the
divisions of the windows, but the
porte-cochere is Gothic and the front
dormer partly so.

2

EUCLID AVENUE 241

3

4

3. Leonard C. Hanna House (1904)
Euclid Avenue east of 27th Street

With this house, a Stanford White
design, Euclid Avenue acquired a
mansion as pretentious as those at
Newport. Leonard Hanna was
associated with his brother Marcus
Hanna in the M. A. Mather Company.
From 1921 until 1957, when it was
demolished, the mansion housed the
Cleveland Museum of Natural History.

4. William Chisholm House (1887)
Euclid Avenue east of 28th Street

Here is another example of
Schweinfurth's Richardsonian manner
in a house smaller and less elaborate
than the Everett mansion. The device
of a group of small windows divided
by colonettes and surrounded by a

sculptured band, found on the side
elevation of the Everett house, is
elaborated here in the gable window.

5. W. H. Boardman House (1893)
Euclid Avenue east of 36th Street
Here, Schweinfurth has used the
Shingle Style in the form most often
associated with the early work of
McKim, Mead and White: a mixture of
Richardsonian and delicate, vaguely
classical, elements.

6. Euclid Avenue, North Side,
Between 24th and 30th Streets
From left to right, the homes of
Samuel Bingham, Harry K. Devereux,
Samuel Mather, Leonard C. Hanna,
and the Hickox-Brown house.

244   EUCLID AVENUE

7. Charles F. Brush House (1884)
Euclid Avenue east of 37th Street

Charles Francis Brush, inventor of the arc lamp, made a fortune from patents and from the manufacture of electrical generating equipment by the Brush Electric Company after 1880. The gable end, with its chimneys connected by a parapet, recalls early Western Reserve brick architecture.

8. Euclid Avenue, North Side, West of 40th Street

From left to right, the homes of Charles F. Brush, T. S. Beckwith, and Jephtha H. Wade.

9. John D. Rockefeller House
Euclid Avenue at 40th Street

John D. Rockefeller married Laura Spelman in 1864. They lived in this house from 1868 until around 1880, when they moved to "Forest Hills," their country home. High Victorian in detail, this is essentially a Tuscan villa with a mansard roof on it. Rockefeller is said to have demolished an adjoining corner house in order to have becomingly spacious grounds.

8

9

10

11

246   EUCLID AVENUE

10. Sylvester T. Everett House (1883) Euclid Avenue at 40th Street

This mansion was built for Sylvester T. Everett, treasurer of the city of Cleveland and an important figure in local financial, industrial, and political circles, and his bride, Alice Louisa Wade, grand-daughter of Jephtha Wade, the early Cleveland industrialist. The grandest house in the city at the time of construction, it was perhaps never outdone. It was also Schweinfurth's first Cleveland commission. It shows his early Richardson Romanesque manner at its very best. It was razed in 1938.

11. Sylvester T. Everett House. This view from the rear of the Everett mansion gives a true impression of its size.

12. Sylvester T. Everett House. The grand staircase, showing the balcony from which Mrs. Everett welcomed guests to her parties as they ascended to the third floor ballroom. Among the guests of the Everetts were Presidents Grant, Hayes, McKinley, and Taft, and industrialists Andrew Carnegie and J. Pierpont Morgan.

13. Jephtha H. Wade House (c. 1870) Euclid Avenue at 40th Street

Jephtha Wade began as a portrait painter, but in 1848 interested himself in the development of the telegraph; through this he became one of Cleveland's wealthiest and most prominent citizens. In this house he entertained President Grant during Grant's visit in 1870. The double stair gives an extra quality of magnificence to this late version of a Tuscan villa.

14

15

14. Euclid Avenue East of 40th
Street, 1900
West of this point streetcars were
diverted from the Avenue.

15. David Z. Norton House (1897–98)
Euclid Avenue at 73rd Street
Schweinfurth designed this house for
one of Cleveland's leading
philanthropists and art patrons. A
native of the city, Norton began a
career in banking at 17 in 1868.
Twenty-two years later, he and Earl
W. Oglebay founded the mining and
shipping firm of Oglebay Norton and
Company, which still exists. By the
time this house was designed,
Schweinfurth had abandoned the
Richardsonian style of his early days
for the Tudor idiom he was to favor
for the rest of his life.

248   *EUCLID AVENUE*

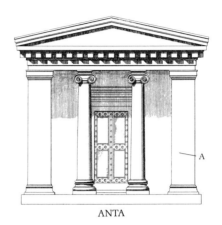
ANTA

GLOSSARY

ADAM, ADAMESQUE. In the style of Robert Adam (1728–92), Scottish architect and designer, characterized by imaginative adaptations of ancient Roman motifs, often so as to yield a light, intricate, and colorful effect.

ANTA (pl. *antae*). A pier, square in plan and having a capital; used to terminate an area of wall in ancient Greek or Roman architecture but sometimes used in the Neoclassical period as a freestanding member in place of a column. Columns placed between antae, as in front of a portico, are said to be *in antis*.

ARCADE. A row of arches with their supporting columns or piers.

ARCH. A structure formed of wedge-shaped stones (*voussoirs*), bricks, or other objects laid so as to maintain one another firmly in position: usually curved upwards but sometimes flat, as over window openings. An upwardly curved head, as over a doorway or window.

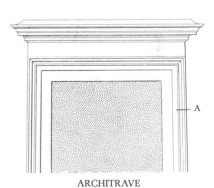
ARCHITRAVE

ARCHITRAVE. The lowest member of a classical entablature, symbolizing a beam laid across the capitals of columns. In a classical doorway or window, a frame suggesting the architrave of such an entablature, continued downward to form jambs.

ASHLAR. Stonework formed of cut rectangular pieces, laid either so as to form continuous courses the entire length of a wall (*coursed ashlar*) or so as to combine stones of varying sizes (*random ashlar*), in either case without thick or irregular mortar joints.

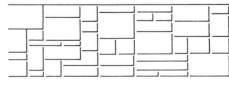
COURSED ASHLAR

BALUSTRADE. A low barrier formed of uprights (*balusters*) supporting a railing.

BARGEBOARD. See *vergeboard*.

RANDOM ASHLAR

BLIND ARCADE. A decorative motif suggesting an arcade that has been walled up: in the Western Reserve and elsewhere, sometimes used, along with a pediment, to decorate the entire front of a Federal-period house.

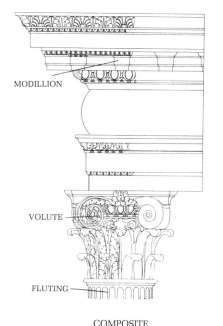

MODILLION

VOLUTE

FLUTING

COMPOSITE

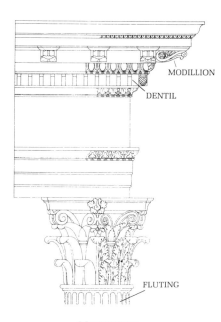

MODILLION

DENTIL

FLUTING

CORINTHIAN

BOX CORNICE. A bulky, hollow cornice concealing a roof gutter and suggesting masonry though usually built in wood.

BRACKET. In Victorian architecture, a symbolic cantilever, usually of fanciful form, used under a cornice in place of the usual mutule or modillion. Popular in the Western Reserve from before 1850 until after 1880, brackets are most characteristic of the Tuscan style of the 1850's, one variety of which, indeed, is known as *Bracketed*.

CANTILEVER. A horizontal structural member supported only at one end; a bracket.

CARPENTER GOTHIC. A style of wooden building characterized by ornamentation in cut-out planking, popular especially in the 1870's and '80's.

CENTERPIECE. A plaster ornament in the center of a ceiling, usually surrounding the place from which a lighting fixture is suspended.

CHANNEL. Any of a series of grooves, immediately joining one another, that form the surface of the shaft of a Doric column.

CLAPBOARD. A horizontal wooden board, tapered at the upper edge and laid so as to cover a portion of a similar board underneath and to be partly covered by a similar one above; used as siding for a wooden building.

CLASSICAL. Noting or pertaining to the architecture of ancient Greece and Rome, or to any architecture based upon these.

COLONIAL. Noting or pertaining to the architecture of the eastern United States while it was still a colonial territory of Great Britain. In ordinary use, the term refers to the architectural style of the Georgian period (1720–80).

COLONNADE. A row of columns, which in classical architecture support an entablature.

COMPOSITE. Noting or pertaining to a Roman order of architecture similar to the Corinthian but having Ionic volutes as one feature of its capital.

CORINTHIAN. Noting or pertaining to a Greek or Roman order of architecture typically characterized by a slender, fluted column with a capital suggesting clustered acanthus leaves, an architrave in three levels, a frieze that is sometimes richly decorated, and a cornice supported by dentils and modillions.

CORNER BLOCK. A block placed at a corner of the casing around a wooden door or window frame, usually treated ornamentally.

CORNER BOARD. A vertical board at the end of a wall that has been covered with wooden siding, used to give the wall a neat edge; sometimes treated as a pilaster or anta.

CORNICE. A decoratively treated horizontal member, originally intended to carry the eaves of a roof beyond the outer surface of a wall but now sometimes used purely as an element of an architectural composition.

CUPOLA. (In Victorian architecture) a lantern on a roof.

DENTIL. Any of a number of small cubical members at the base of an Ionic, Corinthian, or Composite cornice.

DORIC. Noting or pertaining to a Greek or Roman order of architecture typically characterized by a stout channeled column (in Grecian Doric, without a base) supporting an entablature consisting of a plain architrave, a frieze consisting of blocks incised vertically (*triglyphs*) and panels which are sometimes ornamented (*metopes*), and a cornice supported by horizontal slabs (*mutules*) which usually have small conical objects (*guttae*) on their undersides.

DORMER. A shelter for a window opening in a sloping roof.

EAVES. The part of a sloping roof that projects beyond a wall.

ECLECTICISM. The borrowing and combining of architectural compositions or decorative motifs characteristic of cultures other than one's own, as in early Victorian architecture in the United States. In late nineteenth and twentieth-century architecture, the movement characterized by such borrowing.

ENTABLATURE. In classical architecture, a triple horizontal member, originally supported by columns, consisting, from bottom to top, of an architrave, symbolizing a beam, a frieze, usually ornamented, and a cornice.

FACADE. A front of a building, especially one treated so as to be beautiful or imposing.

FANLIGHT. An overdoor light, usually arched, whose tracery suggests an opened fan.

FASCIA BOARD. See *frieze board*.

FENESTRATION. The arrangement of windows and other openings in a building.

FESTOON. An ornament in the form of a garland of flowers, a string of fruit, or a piece of drapery suspended between two points so as to sag gently in the middle; a swag.

FILLET. A small, flat, raised surface. See also under *fluting*.

FLEMISH BOND. An arrangement of bricks on a wall surface such that the bricks in any course show sides and ends alternately, with a side in any course having an end above and below it, and vice-versa.

FLUSH SIDING. (In a wooden building) siding which lies in a single plane.

FLUTING. A system of vertical grooves (*flutes*) in the shaft of an Ionic, Corinthian, or Composite column. Fluting differs from the Doric channeling in that portions of the cylindrical surface of the column (*fillets*) separate the flutes.

FRENCH ROOF. A mansard roof, especially one having very steep sides and a flat or nearly flat upper area.

FRETWORK. An ornamental pattern, usually geometrical and symmetrical about two axes crossing at right angles, used singly or repeatedly to fill a panel.

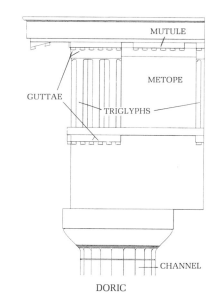

MUTULE

METOPE

GUTTAE

TRIGLYPHS

CHANNEL

DORIC

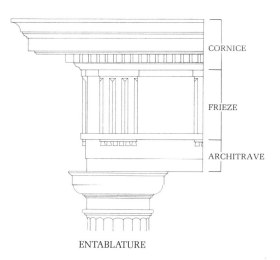

CORNICE

FRIEZE

ARCHITRAVE

ENTABLATURE

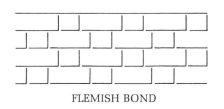

FLEMISH BOND

FRETWORK

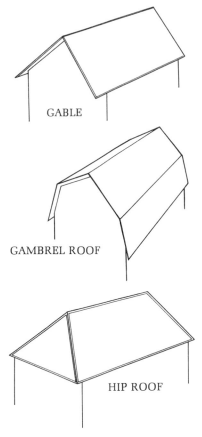

GABLE

GAMBREL ROOF

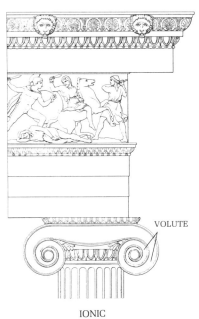

HIP ROOF

IONIC

VOLUTE

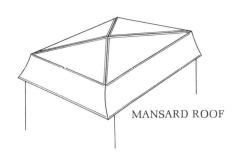

MANSARD ROOF

FRIEZE. The intermediate member of a classical entablature, usually ornamented. A horizontal decorative panel.

FRIEZE BOARD. The frieze of an entablature built of wood.

FRONTPIECE. In old builder's handbooks, an entrance, with its architectural frame.

GABLE. An area of wall under one end of a sloping roof.

GABLE ROOF. A roof with rectangular surfaces, ordinarily two in number, and a ridge.

GAMBREL ROOF. A gable roof, more or less symmetrical, having four inclined surfaces, the pair meeting at the ridge having the shallower pitch.

GOTHIC. Noting, pertaining to, or in the style of the architecture of the late Middle Ages, characterized by pointed arches, vertical lines, and often by elaborate decorative work.

GUTTAE. See under *Doric*.

HIP ROOF. A roof without gables, each of whose sides, ordinarily four in number, lies in a single plane and joins the others at an apex or ridge.

IN ANTIS. See under *anta*.

IONIC. Noting or pertaining to a Greek or Roman order of architecture typically characterized by a slender, fluted column with a low capital having projecting volutes, an architrave in three levels, a shallow frieze that is sometimes ornamented, and a cornice that is sometimes supported by dentils.

LANTERN. A structure raised above a roof or dome to admit light to a space below.

LINTEL. A horizontal member spanning an opening and supporting a load; a beam.

MANSARD ROOF. A modification of the hipped roof in which each side has two planes, the upper one being the shallower; French roof.

MEETING HOUSE. A building for Protestant worship. Used mainly at present to refer to such a building for the Society of Friends.

MODILLION. A small, bracket-like member immediately underneath a cornice, found especially in the Corinthian and Composite orders.

MOLDING. A relatively long, shallow member, usually decorative, either uniform in cross section or bearing a pattern in low relief, used for various purposes, as to divide a wall area, emphasize an opening, cast a shadow, give an effect of slenderness to a thick architectural member, or shed rain water running down a wall.

MULLION. A vertical member dividing a window area and forming part of the window frame.

MUNTIN. A molding forming part of the frame of a window sash and holding one side of a pane.

MUTULE. See under *Doric*.

NAVE. The central area of a church, occupied by the congregation.

OVERDOOR LIGHT. A glazed area above a doorway, often decoratively treated.

PALLADIAN. Noting or pertaining to the refined, symmetrical, and often austere architecture of Andrea Palladio (1518–80) and his followers.

PALLADIAN MOTIF. A motif often used in eighteenth-century work, consisting of a broad opening with a semicircular arch for a head and two narrower side compartments having flat heads at the level of the springing of the arch. Used especially as a form of window (*Palladian window*).

PARAPET. A low wall above the roof surface of a building, directly over its outer wall.

PEDIMENT. A triangular gable bounded on all sides by continuations of a cornice. An ornamental member over a doorway or window that has the general form of such a gable.

PENDANT. A hanging decorative member.

PILASTER. A flat decorative member, applied to a wall, whose form suggests a column.

QUOIN. A squared stone used to reinforce the corner of a masonry building. A decorative feature in this form, used to give emphasis to the corner of a building.

ROMANESQUE. Noting, pertaining to, or in the style of the architecture of the Middle Ages immediately before the Gothic, characterized by massive construction using the semicircular arch.

ROTUNDA. A building or area of a building covered by a dome.

SHINGLE STYLE. A primarily residential style developed in the United States in the late Victorian period, characterized by informal planning, bold massing, and the extensive use of shingles as a siding.

SIDELIGHT. A narrow window area beside an outside door, common in Federal and Greek Revival work.

SOFFIT. The underside of a cornice, arch, lintel, etc. Distinguished from a ceiling by its relatively small area.

STEPPED GABLE. A gable concealing the end of a roof with a stepped parapet.

SWAG. A festoon, especially a heavy one.

TOWN HOUSE. A masonry house whose plan allows other houses to adjoin it immediately.

TRACERY. An ornamental division of an opening, especially a large window, in the form of an arrangement of mullions, arches, etc.

TUSCAN. Noting or pertaining to an order of Roman architecture,

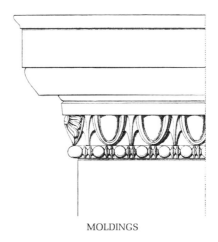

MOLDINGS

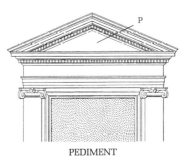

PEDIMENT

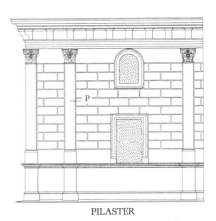

PALLADIAN MOTIF

PILASTER

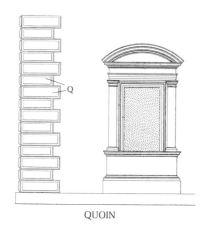

QUOIN

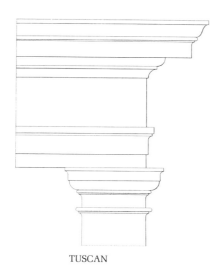

TUSCAN

typically having a stout, unfluted and unchanneled column with a capital similar to the Doric and a plain architrave, plain frieze, and simple, widely jutting cornice. Noting or pertaining to a mainly residential style of American architecture of the 1850's and somewhat later, characterized by plain, cubical massing, flaring cornices supported by brackets with fanciful forms, and cupolas serving as staircase lanterns or as elevated rooms.

VERGEBOARD. A wooden member, usually treated decoratively, suspended from and following the slopes of a gable roof; bargeboard.

VERNACULAR. Noting or pertaining to construction whose appearance reflects local popular taste or the limitations of local resources of building materials, workmanship, etc.

VICTORIAN. Noting or pertaining to the architecture common in the reign of Queen Victoria (1837–1901). In ordinary use, the term refers to that from c. 1850 to c. 1880, characterized by Gothic, Italian, and French influence.

VOLUTE. An ornamental spiral, as that at either end of an Ionic capital.

VOUSSOIR. See under *arch*.

BIBLIOGRAPHY

This bibliography is for those who would like to explore further the nineteenth-century architecture of the Western Reserve and its historic background. It is not a comprehensive reading list, but at the same time, it is a somewhat specialized one. A number of general histories of American architecture—though alas, none of Ohio architecture—exist, each with its shortcomings. There are, for example, Wayne Andrews' *Architecture, Ambition, and Americans;* James Marston Fitch's *American Building: The Historical Forces that Shaped It;* Oliver Larkin's *Art and Life in America;* John E. Burchard and Albert Bush-Brown's *The Architecture of America;* and Henry-Russell Hitchcock's *Architecture: Nineteenth and Twentieth Centuries.* The most objective and factual is the Hitchcock book, but this is a general history of the period, taking in Europe as well as America. Some such book can give the reader general background information, after which he can use the list below to follow up any special interests.

No comprehensive list of nineteenth-century builder's guides and plan books can be given. The Samuel Sloan book, listed mainly because of its probable influence on a Western Reserve church, stands for many such publications, large and small, that appeared throughout the nineteenth century. Many public libraries have a few examples, which, along with similar books—ironfounder's catalogues, for example—can give the reader a fascinating evening.

A number of classics in the area of nineteenth-century American architecture, both old builder's guides and later books on the architecture of the period, have been reissued by Dover Publications, Inc., 180 Varick Street, New York, N.Y. 10014, and by the Da Capo Press, 227 West 17th Street, New York, N.Y. 10011. Reprint editions available at the end of 1970 are listed.

BENJAMIN, ASHER. *The American Builder's Companion: or, A System of Architecture Particularly Adapted to the Present Style of Building.* First edition, Boston, 1806. Dover reprint of sixth (1827) edition, with new introduction by William Morgan, 1969.

An important builder's guide, basically Federal or even late Georgian, but with a short section on "Grecian Architecture" in the 1827 edition.

Other Benjamin works include *The Rudiments of Architecture* (1814), *The Practical House Carpenter* (1830), *The Practice of Architecture* (1833), *The Builder's Guide* (1839), and *The Elements of Architecture* (1843). Each appeared in several editions.

BUTLER, MARGARET MANOR. *A Pictorial History of the Western Reserve: 1796 to 1860.* Cleveland: The Early Settlers Association of the Western Reserve and the Western Reserve Historical Society, 1963.

Many pictures of Western Reserve buildings, demolished and existing.

CHAPMAN, EDMUND H. *Cleveland: Village to Metropolis.* Cleveland: The Western Reserve Historical Society and The Press of Case Western Reserve University, 1964.

Described as "a case study of problems of urban development in nineteenth-century America," this book discusses the development of Cleveland up to around 1880. Many good photographs of mansions, churches, and commercial buildings now gone.

DOWNING, ANDREW JACKSON. *The Architecture of Country Houses.* First edition, New York, 1850. Dover reprint, with introduction by J. Stewart Johnson, 1969.

A variety of designs for rural houses large and small, mainly in the Gothic Revival and Tuscan styles, along with practical advice on decoration, furnishing, construction, heating and ventilation, etc. Of interest also are Downing's *Cottage Residences: A Series of Designs for Rural Cottages* (1842) and *A Treatise on the Theory and Practice of Landscape Gardening . . . With Remarks on Rural Architecture* (1841).

EASTLAKE, CHARLES L. *Hints on Household Taste.* First edition, London, 1868. Dover reprint of fourth (1878) edition, with introduction by John Gloag, 1969.

Although English, this book, intended to effect a rational reform in furnishings and decoration, had a considerable influence in the United States in the late Victorian period. Many illustrations.

FRARY, I. T. *Early Homes of Ohio.* Richmond, 1936. Dover reprint, 1970.

Covers the entire state of Ohio through the Greek Revival period, concentrating on houses but giving some attention to churches, courthouses, and business buildings as well. Approximately 200 photographs.

HAMLIN, TALBOT. *Greek Revival Architecture in America.* London and New York: Oxford University Press, 1944. Dover reprint, 1964.

An excellent, wide-ranging account of Greek Revival architecture in all parts of the United States, which discusses its most important designers, the development of its forms, the builder's guides of the period, and the cultural background of the American people that allowed the Greek Revival to develop and spread. Ninety-four plates, mostly with several illustrations apiece.

HATCHER, HARLAN. *The Western Reserve: The Story of New Connecticut in Ohio.* Second edition, Cleveland and New York: World Publishing Co., 1966.

HITCHCOCK, ELIZABETH G. "Charles Wallace Heard (1806–1876) Architect: His Buildings in Cleveland and Painesville," in *The Historical Society Quarterly, Lake County, Ohio,* IX, No. 1 (February 1967).

HORTON, JOHN J. *The Jonathan Hale Farm: A Chronicle of the Cuyahoga Valley.* Cleveland: The Western Reserve Historical Society, 1961.

A factual account of the history of a farm in the Western Reserve from its settlement in 1810 through the first third of the present century. The house is shown in the Summit County section of this book.

JOHANNESEN, ERIC. *Ohio College Architecture Before 1870.* Columbus, Ohio: The Ohio Historical Society, 1969.

A brief illustrated history covering the entire state. This is the first of the Ohio Historical Society's "Historic Ohio Buildings" series.

———. "Simeon Porter," in *Ohio History* (1965), Vol. 74, No. 3.

KIMBALL, FISKE. *Domestic Architecture of the American Colonies and of the Early Republic.* New York, 1922. Dover reprint, 1966.

A well-illustrated survey of Colonial and Federal architecture along the United States seaboard, with some attention to the Greek Revival.

LAFEVER, MINARD. *The Beauties of Modern Architecture.* New York, 1835. Da Capo reprint, with new introduction by Denys Peter Myers, 1968.

Contains original designs of great beauty and refinement as well as the measured drawings from authentic Greek examples standard in builder's guides of this period. Forty-eight plates.

———. *The Modern Builder's Guide.* First edition. New York, 1833. Dover reprint, with new introduction by Jacob Landy and three added plates, 1969.

Original designs for exterior and interior details; church elevations; plans, elevations, and sections of a large villa; diagrams for laying out vaults and stair railings and for solving other difficult geometrical problems; and a copious text. Other books by Lafever are *The Young Builder's General Instructor* (1829) and *The Architectural Instructor* (1856); the latter is a product of Lafever's eclectic period.

MUMFORD, LEWIS. *The Brown Decades: A Study of the Arts in America, 1865–1895.* New York, 1931. Dover reprint, 1955.

A survey of mid- and late-Victorian architecture, figurative arts, and literature.

PIERSON, WILLIAM H. *American Buildings and Their Architects: The Colonial and Neo-Classical Styles.* New York: Doubleday and Co., 1970.

Very interesting and informative.

SCHUYLER, MONTGOMERY. American Architecture *and Other Writings of Montgomery Schuyler.* Edited by Ralph Coe. Cambridge, Mass.: Belknap Press of Harvard University Press, 1961.

Highly interesting, particularly on the Queen Anne style and on the Chicago exposition of 1893, the first great display of the classicism that characterized official, commercial, and to some extent domestic, architecture in the United States.

SCULLY, VINCENT. *The Shingle Style*. New Haven: Yale University Press, 1955.

An excellent study of the revolution in domestic architecture brought about by Richardson and others in the late 1870's and early 1880's. Many photographs, engravings, and plans.

SLOAN, SAMUEL. *The Model Architect*. Philadelphia, 1852 and 1860.

A lavishly illustrated work by an influential Philadelphia architect, showing the eclecticism of the years before the Civil War. This was a time when the development of lithography encouraged the publication of highly ambitious architectural folios, some of which, as is the case here, include full-color plates.

VAN RENSSELAER, MARIANA GRISWOLD. *Henry Hobson Richardson and His Works*. Cambridge, Mass., 1888. Dover reprint, with new introduction by William Morgan, 1969.

A life of Richardson and an appreciation of his work, illustrated with early photographs and line drawings, including some of Richardson's sketches.

COMMUNITIES HAVING BUILDINGS
ILLUSTRATED IN THIS BOOK